T
To Living your Dreams!

# If

# Relationships Were Like Sports, Men Would at Least Know the

# Score

Blessings,

Dr. Monty

# If

# Relationships Were Like Sports, Men Would at Least Know the Score

by

Dr. Marty Finkelstein

For everyone who has been in a relationship, is presently in a relationship, or will eventually be in a relationship.

Sol-Rose Publications

4292 D. Memorial Drive

Decatur, Ga. 30032

ISBN 1-58500-651-3

Book cover design Virginia Gilleland

1stBooks - rev. 02/18/00

Other books by Dr. Marty Finkelstein :

- *A Life of Wellness*- Guidelines for avoiding Illness
- *For the Love of the Game*- Tennis, mind body, peak performance
- *8 Lessons for Life on Hole 1* – A story about a boy, golf, and the human spirit
- *Poetry and Songs*- Moments in Time

I believe all life's experiences occur for a reason to teach us something deep in our soul that brings us closer to God.

Sometimes it is difficult to know what the lesson is at the moment.

Dedicated to

Every relationship

That has been my teacher

And to God

Who has always

Shown me

The path of learning and loving

And improving

My batting average.

# Contents

## Acknowledgments

My deepest appreciation to the following people who have contributed directly or indirectly to this book, and to those people who have never stopped believing in me, even when I was in a slump.

Shae Bennett for her dedicated assistance managing to read through my scribbled pages, and transform them into the computer and for her help with on-going editing. This she did in the evening after working in my office during the day. Brian Bennett for his creative support and assistance in the design of the book. April Boozer for her dedicated spirit who helped to type this manuscript at night while running my office during the day. Debra Crowe whose friendship and home on the beach was a wonderful retreat for me to write, meditate, and share insightful conversations, while watching the sunrise. Dr. Louis Leonardi for his ongoing friendship, support, assistance, and encouragement inspiring me to fulfill my dreams.

Dr. Michael Norwood for his ongoing friendship, assistance, and for contributing to the concept of relationship athletics. Kevin Virgilio Colbert for her continuous love and friendship for over twenty-five years, and for listening for hours while I read through the first draft of this book. Alan Gathercoal for his friendship, encouragement and continued support. Mattie Keane for her inspiration, wonderful heart, devoted editing, and assistance in manifesting my vision. Barbara Mickelson for her wonderful support and assistance and helpful editing. Gary Ivey for his helpful editing. Virginia Gilleland for her inspirations and love and sharing the sun and moon with me. Dr. Kathryn Lawson my ex-wife and lifetime friend and mother of our two wonderful children. Thank you for continuing to play with me, and sharing our lives. Dr. David Finkelstein my brother, Molly his wife, and Alex and Ellie my nephew and niece, whose love support and home on Martha's Vineyard was a perfect oasis to write and share my vision. Louis Finkelstein my dad who at seventy-seven still pursues his dreams like a twenty-seven year old and inspires us all to live passionately each day. Julia and Nathaniel, my children who give me the wondrous blessings of being a dad, that fill me with joy each moment.

# Introduction

The purpose of this book is to create a playful way for couples to discover how they can improve relationships while having fun. Anyone who has been in a romantic relationship knows how difficult it can be to sustain the initial passion and excitement, as the relationship matures giving way to mutual respect and intimacy. In one sense it seems it should be so easy to have the relationship of our dreams, where we are being fully expressed emotionally, physically, and spiritually, yet at times it feels like we are not even on the same playing field as our partner, playing by the same rules, or using the same equipment. And that is precisely how the title of this book became manifested. Maybe it doesn't have to be as complicated as it has become, if we simply learn how to keep score with one another, and understand the same rules. So often we don't have the slightest clue when it comes to evaluating the relationship we are in and knowing the score. In a time when fifty percent of marriages end in divorce, words like commitment and promise and vows can mean different things to various people.

When we enter relationships blindly hoping that this time it is going to be different, yet not knowing how to make it different, it is a lot like playing golf in total darkness. Perhaps hitting the initial drive may not be so difficult, but finding the ball can be a tedious journey, while we hope somehow, the ball will magically discover the green and jump in the hole. Even the most masterful golfers would not venture to play under these circumstances.

I believe the reason so many people love sports, and are drawn to participate in them as well as observe them, is because of their simplicity. We understand that a baseball game has three outs to an inning, and typically nine innings a game. And, we appreciate the rules in baseball will not be the same rules in football even though they are both sports. Of course a clear distinction between sports and relationships is what constitutes winning. In sports, the object is to out score your opponent, so that you are victorious. Also the purpose is to improve your own game to the highest level of excellence so that you are always seeking your own mastery of the game. In relationships, winning is when you and your partner are elevated to a higher level of romance, respect, intimate communication, and playfulness. In relationships if you are winning at your partner's expense, the relationship is losing. Your partner is on the same team as you, and scoring only occurs when it is beneficial for the whole team.

Personally I didn't choose to write this book. In some mysterious way it chose me. And since the book came through me as if I were a vessel to be spoken through, I, too, became the book's student and discovered that I had not been playing the game as masterfully as I could. And yet, the true discovery was finding how easy it could be to create extraordinary relationships, relationships that could evolve into a lifetime of trust and intimacy, with the joyous celebration of each other.

So often, I have felt I was just getting warmed up. Just one more inning and I'd be in my player's zone. Just one more chance at the foul line and I'd win the game, only to find the game was already over.

How often have we all seen a baseball coach walk out to the mound when the pitcher is wearing a look of frustration, after giving up three runs. The pitcher knows he's in trouble and we can only imagine the conversation.

Coach:   It's not looking good.
          Pitcher:  I'm just getting warmed up.
          They hit some good pitches.
They just got lucky.
I know I can get the next batters.

Coach:   Sorry kid, it'll have to be another day.
We're already bringing in Lefty.

And so it is with relationships. Women are always keeping score, remembering every error, or misshot, and men are always wanting one more inning, one more serve, one more hole, only to discover the game has been over. You fouled out, regardless of your twenty-five points. As the title of the book suggests, men need to learn how to keep score and know what the score is in the relationship. There is nothing more heart breaking than losing when you thought you were winning, and nothing more confusing then winning when you thought you had lost.

Once I was playing in a doubles tennis match.  The games went on for a couple of hours, and after a long rally, one of the players on the other team walked toward the net, so I did the same walking toward him. He proceeded to reach out his hand to shake mine, and said "Good game". In which I honestly and amusingly replied "Who won?" He looked at me perplexed and said, "You did." I turned toward my partner and said, "We won." Though both of us thought we were down a set.  As we walked off the court laughing in bewilderment, our only thought was that we all had been abducted by aliens for awhile.

Well the good news is; that does not occur in sports too often, yet the bad news is, it can occur all too often in relationships. How often is the question asked by a friend when a relationship ends,

"What happened?  I thought everything was great. You both seemed like such a wonderful couple."

The reply can be,

"I'm not certain what happened. I had just purchased tickets for us to go to the Bahamas where I was going to propose.  I thought we had a wonderful night last night, we even made love. In the morning, when I awoke, she was already gone to work. I was getting ready to leave and there at the door were my clothes and my toothbrush in a large paper bag with a note that said, "Sorry kid, I'm bringing in Lefty with the curveball. Your stuff was wearing off." And as I walked out to my car, I could have sworn I was pitching great and had a few good innings left in the game. Maybe it's just a practical joke I thought, or maybe I'm dreaming, or perhaps I've been abducted by aliens! But whatever it is, I don't know what happened!"

# How to Read the Book

The book is divided into three sections:

1. Beginning and Evaluating the game.
2. Playing the Game which is divided into five sports; Baseball, Basketball, Golf, Tennis, and Football.
3. Ending the Game, and discovering new games to begin.

Each sport has its own unique scoring system, and specific characteristics and terminology that act as playful and insightful metaphors for aiding in the development and interaction within relationships. It is recommended you read one sport at a time, before going on to the next sport. And to use the book as a workbook when it is suggested. I hope you discover when you begin applying these simple suggestions to improving your relationship, that not only is the process meaningful and enjoyable, but that the relationship is brought to a new level of passion, understanding, and love.

As you are learning how to score in your relationship, you will also discover that regardless of whether you are on your first date, in a steady relationship, or with someone you are married to; the same rules will apply.

## How to Play the Game

### "Relationship Athletics"

This is a book that is also a game. Most couples love to play games together. Some play card games, others play board games; there are hundreds of games that couples enjoy. Well, this book is designed to have couples play a game that will make the efforts they put into relationships so satisfying that they will never want to stop playing these games with each other. Communication will improve. Understanding will improve. Mutual trust will improve. Intimacy, and lovemaking will only get better.

After each section of every sport there is a scorecard. After you, as a couple, have read the book, it is suggested that for one week you both pick one sport to play together. It is absolutely necessary to play one sport at a time before going on to the next sport. Most relationships fail because two people are playing two different sports, and wondering why it is so difficult to communicate. Each day the man will fill in his scorecard evaluating how he believes he has done. At the same time, his partner will fill in her scorecard evaluating how she believes her partner has done. At the end of the day go over the score with each other while having fun sharing with one another. At the end of one week discover the intimate wonderful changes in the relationship and choose your next sport.

## Guidelines to Playing the Game

- Play one sport at a time

1- Choose a time of day when both of you are relaxed and can look forward to playing the game with each other.

2- Ideally, you have no distractions and are looking forward to communicating with each other.

3- Approach the scoring in a fun way, remembering the goal of the game is for the relationship to improve and for you to discover new insights with each other.

4- Men, listen with an open mind to how your partner has scored you. Your goal is not to be argumentative when you discover you committed a foul, even when you thought it was a great dunk.

5- Write down your scores daily and total your points at the end of the week.

Discover how you can score points during the week, so that the relationship is consistently winning, while you are having fun.

6- Discover ways of scoring points that are different from the traditional points you have scored before. Example: Create assists and new singles and fairway shots that are unique for you. You will understand once you read the book.

7- Start a new game at the end of the week and follow the same guidelines.

8- Continue to play the game.

" We haven't failed.We now know a thousand things that won't work so we're that much closer to finding what will."

Thomas A. Edison
Regarding his inventions


" A man is measured by how much pressure he can bare. You can't imprison yourself with self doubt, you've got to have confidence in whatever you do."

Evander Holyfield
Heavy Weight Boxing Champion

# 1

# Beginning the Game

# Self Evaluation Check List

All great athletes manifest specific qualities and skills and they are always seeking to improve their optimum performance and potential. Whether it is Barry Bonds, Muhammed Ali, Monaca Seles, Tiger Woods, Martina Hingis, or Michael Jordan, these qualities manifest into their success.

In relationships you can evaluate yourself by observing how these qualities are reflected in your life and how your relationships are improving as these skills improve.

### 1- Vision

What is your vision for your life and your relationship with your partner? The clearer the vision the more possibilities of manifesting success.

### 2- Positive Mental Attitude

How you are responding to life's curve balls and fast balls? Determine the potential of developing healthy evolving relationships.

### 3- Flexibility

Evaluate your ability to be flexible in response to new thoughts and ideas and to your willingness to be open to your partner's communication. Observe your capacity to compromise and bend when necessary.

### 4- Resiliency

Evaluate your ability to bounce back after disagreements or

arguments or upsets in life. Does it take you years, months, days, or minutes?

### 5- Timing

Evaluate your sense of timing in relationships. There is a proper time for beginning a relationship, a proper time for communication, rest, fun, lovemaking, and silence.

### 6- Balance

Evaluate your sense of balance in the relationship. Are you making your health, your career, your family, and your partner all-important in your life?

### 7- Endurance

Evaluate your ability to sustain your love and energy through the many passages of life, and the intimate development of your relationship.

### 8- Concentration

Evaluate your ability to keep your focus on the things that are most important, so that the little things do not distract you.

### 9- Fun

Evaluate your sense of enjoyment and fun in the relationship. Discover the ability to enjoy the simple things in life.

### 10- Inner and outer strength

Evaluate your commitment and determination to follow through with your promises and to see your visions fulfilled.

## 11- Love

Evaluate your ability to bring your love and passion into the relationship with the desire to know the person you are with in the deepest, most tender way.

**All great athletes manifest these qualities!**

# Evaluating other Teams or Players in Sports

## Scouting Report

In sports, coaches, managers, and players develop an insightful understanding of the skills and talents, the strengths and weaknesses of their own team. When Michael Jordan was asked why he still practices so much before a game, his simple reply was, " I still know where my game can improve."

If the best in the world ever can get better, that can certainly humble the rest of us to understanding there is always room to improve our talents. Once a player, or team, determines his own level of excellence, then the goal is to determine the other team, or players' weaknesses and strengths. We would assume that if Andre Agassi and Peter Sampras were playing each other in a tennis match, that they would know everything they could about each other before beginning the match.

### Evaluations in sports

First, evaluate yourself.

Second, evaluate your opponent.

1- Know your opponents' strengths, and weaknesses.
2- Understand their strategy and mental game.
3- Watch videos and observe.
4- Know their style.
5- What has been their past record against other teams or players, or against yourself?
6- Know the playing field, or court, or course you are on.
7- Determine your own game plan.
8- Has the team, or a particular player been improving their game this season?
9- How does the player or team deal with stress?

## Evaluating Potential Partners in Relationships

Foremost, it is important that you understand and know what you desire most in a relationship and what qualities you believe to be your strengths to empower a passionate loving relationship. Just like in sports you want to know the areas in your life that need improvement and to be aware of the wonderful talents that you are already mastering or learning more about. It is essential that you are clear about what values are the most necessary for you in a relationship and what behaviors of the other person may not be acceptable, to even begin the game.

So many errors and strikeouts, fumbles and missed shots can be avoided if you are playing with a partner on the same playing field, using the same equipment, and sharing the same visions. And when you share similar qualities and skills you can empower the relationship to move forward, even when it slices off into the rough of life. Too often people match up with each other in areas that can't endure the length of the game. You may be physically attracted to someone because you like how she looks in tennis shorts and you like her serve. She may be attracted to you for your fancy golf shoes, and your follow-through stroke. But, if she is consistently playing tennis and you are consistently playing golf, problems will eventually occur since each game has its own unique style and rules. As an example; tennis has rigid lines that constitute what is in and what is out. In golf, players for the most part, go where the ball goes, even if it is in the woods.

As you keep your score cards in this book, you'll discover that when you play golf with each other, learning how to be in the rough, and manifesting awakenings in the woods is possible. Both partners should be willing to explore these areas of their relationship. But when you are playing tennis together, an out is clearly out. You may say " Wasn't the shot close?"

And she'll reply,

" but it was out."

Since each game is different, with different rules, and different styles, communication will be vastly unique in each sport.

If you are playing golf and she is playing tennis, and you're hoping that someday she'll be a golfer when she is already communicating,

" I don't play golf."

And she is wondering when you're going to hit the tennis ball back to her instead of slicing it out of bounds all the time; it's only a matter of time until she finds a tennis player, regardless of how good your golf clubs look.

### Evaluations for your potential or present partner

### Scouting Report

Be willing to share your self-evaluation with your partner.

### 1.      Know about your partner's record in past relationships.

As in sports any player can go from first to last and last to first, but one's history is vital in determining potential. All of us are on a spiritual path in some form or shape, desiring to improve. We all want our weaknesses to become stronger and our strengths to become wiser. When you know about your partner's past relationships and the choices she has made in those relationships, you are able to see at what level of skill she has been playing. Men can be very naïve when they think that certain non-attractive qualities will change simply because now that person is with them.

A-      Was your partner married? How many times?

    1-      How many other significant relationships?
    2-      What happened?
    3-      What errors did your partner commit?
    4-      Was she monogamous in those relationships?
    5-      Was she trustworthy and honest?
    6-      How did she respond to the loss of the relationship?
    7-      What is the relationship she has with her past partners?

B-      Does your partner have children? How many?

    1-      What is the relationship with her children?
    2-      If she doesn't live with her children, how often does she spend time with them?

C-      Has she ever been with a married man before?

## 2.      How has your partner grown from her past relationships?

    a-      What workshops or seminars has she attended? What was her experience?
    b-      What books has she read and applied?
    c-      How has religion or spiritual teaching assisted her in her life?

d-    Has she traveled? Where? What was her experience?

**3.   How is your partner's relationship with her family? Mom? Dad? Brothers? Sisters?**

**4.   What has been her communication style in relationships?**

a-    Does she express her feelings easily, communicating when errors or fouls, singles and touchdowns have occurred? Or does she withhold emotions, suppressing her feelings?

b-    If she withholds information and effective communication, is it because it is uncomfortable for her, or does she feel it is not important for her to share her inner most feelings?

c-    Does she feel that expressing her feelings is a form of complaining rather than sharing? If your partner does not like to feel like she is complaining, she may withhold communication. Then, when you get a penalty or foul you may be unclear as to why you were ejected from the game.

d-    Does she just expect you to know when you have struck out or double faulted?

**( It is imperative to be on the same playing field to have effective communication that will empower the relationship.)**

**5.** **What is her career style?**

    a-    What type of work does she do?
    b-    Does she enjoy her work?
    c-    How does she respond to the stress at work?
    d-    What are her goals in her career?
    e-    How important is her career to her?

**6.** **What is her spiritual style?**

    a-    Does she belong to an organized religion?
    b-    Does she follow specific spiritual teachings?
    c-    How does she bring her spiritual teachings into her lifestyle? Prayer, meditation, rituals, customs, holidays, retreats, work, play?

**7.** **What is her wellness style?**

    a-    What is she presently doing to manifest a healthy lifestyle?
    b-    How has she changed in her approach to her health from the past?
    c-    Nutrition-What is her understanding of healthy eating?
    d-    Exercise- Is there a specific exercise routine? Does she participate in sports or outdoor activities?
    e-    What are her health goals, and her approach to her health? Is she holistically oriented or more traditional in her approach?

f-      What does she enjoy doing when she is
        not working?

**8.      What is her sexual style?**

If the relationship is not yet a sexual one, then what is her style of expressing affection and compassion and tenderness?

a-      Does she enjoy sex? How does your
        partner express her tenderness?

b-      Does your partner enjoy her body and
        freely express herself to you?

c-      Is your partner vulnerable and open to
        explore the relationship both physically
        and spiritually through sexual intimacy?

d-      How often does your partner like to
        have sex?

e-      Does your partner communicate openly
        about what she enjoys while desiring to
        know what pleases you?

**9.      What is her idea of a wonderful relationship?**

a-      What qualities, that are special, does she
        feel she brings to a relationship?

b-      What is she looking for in a man?

c-      What is her vision of the future?

**10.     What does she consider to be her strengths
        and her weaknesses?**

**Can you admire her strengths and love and support her weaknesses, knowing that her weaknesses may or may not ever change? Can you respect and love the differences between you both? Or will you be fixated to try to change your partner?**

**It is important that you know what differences or weaknesses in a partner are ones that are not acceptable to you.**

Question-

1-    What qualities, characteristics, habits, physical traits, or backgrounds are unacceptable for you to begin a relationship with someone?

Write a paragraph describing a wonderful partner.

It is important to understand that the qualities you desire in your partner should ideally reflect the qualities you are also aspiring for yourself. If you want your partner to be someone who is energetic, successful, healthy then these qualities should reflect what you are radiating as well.

As the story between two young men lamenting about relationships suggests:

**1ˢᵗ man-** Yes, I've been searching for my perfect partner. I thought I was with her, but then I found out she lied to me and I realized, it couldn't be her. Then I believed, it was the next relationship I was in, but when she stopped exercising and keeping trim, I realized it wasn't her. And then finally, I found her. She was everything I was looking for. She was beautiful, intelligent, athletic, artistic, creatively inspiring, and fully expressed in life. She was my perfect mate.

**2ⁿᵈ man-** Well, what happened to her then?

**1ˢᵗ man-** Pause....... Well, ironically she was looking for her perfect partner!

Greg Maddux, four-time Cy Young award winning pitcher for the Atlanta braves, evaluates every hitter that he pitches to. He knows what his past record is with them, what their strengths and weaknesses are, what their hitting percentage is coming into the game, where they like the pitch to be, and where they don't. He knows if they are fastball hitters, or curve ball hitters, as well as knowing their mental toughness and concentration at the plate. He knows if they typically swing at the first pitch, or let the first pitch go by. Of course what makes Maddux so great, and one of the overall best pitchers ever, is that he knows all this information before facing the batter, and then he has the skill and talent to throw the ball exactly where he desires. He keeps perfecting his mastery. And, that is what this book is about, perfecting our mastery in the sport of relationships, the most important sport of our lives.

# PLAYING THE GAME

*"In order to be a good pitcher, you've got to think like a hitter. Why do you think I sit beside our hitting coach every game, when I'm not pitching? It ain't because I like him so much."*

**Greg Maddux**

**Pitcher**

# BASEBALL

*"You have to respect the game. No player is bigger than the game, either go home or play – mistakes made are nothing but it's a mistake not to try."*

**Bobby Cox**
**Manager of Atlanta Braves**

*" I just go out and play and have fun. I don't think about anything but trying to help the ball club win any way I can."*

**Ken Griffey Jr.**
**Baseball Star**

# BASEBALL

| 1 | 2 | 3 | 4 | 5 | 6 | 7 | 8 | 9 |
|---|---|---|---|---|---|---|---|---|
|   |   |   |   |   |   |   |   |   |
|   |   |   |   |   |   |   |   |   |

1- Singles/Hits

2- Errors

3- Homeruns

4- Triples

5- Strikeouts

6- Batting Average/Pitcher's ERA

7-Wild Pitches

8- Slumps

9- Sacrifice Bunts

*"Friday I hit a homerun and we lost; today I had two hits and we won. I feel better today."*

**Sammy Sosa**

### 1- Singles/ Hits

This is the nuts and bolts of the game. In baseball any manager will tell you he needs runners on base to score runs. Hits and singles are the way to accomplish this. In baseball, a single does not have to be impressive. The main goal is to get to first base. Once a runner is on first, then the next batter can hit a single, and then there are runners in scoring position. One more single and you've scored. In baseball a single can be a line drive deep into the outfield or it can be a classy bunt in front of home plate or it can be a grounder that just slips between short stop and third base. They all equal singles and singles are the most effective hit in the game. Coaches are always looking for consistent single hitters. When singles score runs, then runs can win the game.

In relationships singles are everything. This is like the circulatory system moving blood through the body, keeping it alive. Singles are the everyday little things that men can easily neglect or forget. Singles always represent possibilities in relationships. When you're hitting singles consistently, there are always runners on base in scoring position. When there are no runners on base, it is difficult to score runs. In relationships, if there are not consistent singles being hit, the relationship will begin to weaken and eventually fall apart. When men are not hitting singles in the relationship, women begin to feel that their partner is just not interested, that he just doesn't care. After awhile your partner may begin to believe that you just don't know how to hit singles, even if you say you desire to hit them. And, eventually, if your singles are lacking, she may begin scouting for a better and more dependable single hitter. Men often tend to ignore hitting singles, thinking that anyone can hit them.

### Possible singles for men to hit in relationships

(Some of these singles may be extra base hits, depending upon your partner and the circumstances.)

1-A phone call during the day to say hello, and how much "I Love You".

2-Daily affection.

3-Waking up in a positive mood, and sharing a tender embrace.

4-Words of inspiration and appreciation (learning to see all the qualities to appreciate about your partner and learning to inspire her.)

5-Listening to requests made by your partner:

a-picking up groceries
b- picking up clothes at the cleaners
c- putting things away
d- cleaning up after messing up
e-
f-
g-

6-Taking care of yourself and not expecting your partner to take care of you.

7-A desire for your partner to be happy and respecting her needs.

8-Understanding when your partner is not feeling well and being compassionate.

9-When your partner is angry or upset, simply listening to her concern, and not trying to fix her, and certainly not getting upset also. Being understanding

10-Making her feel as if she is the most important person in your life.

11-Your own cleanliness and hygiene

12- Being someone she feels she can depend upon when she needs to: That you are there to take care of her even if she is very capable and powerful in her life.

Add your own singles.

1-

2-

3-

4-

5-

Talk to your partner and find out what would be singles for her, and add those.

1-

2-

3-

4-

5-

Singles win games and singles create lasting wonderful relationships. Women are attracted to home-run hitters, but they want to share their lives with consistent single hitters.

## The Importance of Hitting Singles

For his wife's birthday he decided to do something wonderful and special. When he came home, his wife greeted him at the door, at which time, he requested she step outside and look up toward the sky. There in bold letters soaring between the clouds on a banner attached to a plane, were the words , **I Love You, My Darling. Happy Birthday.**

His wife began to cry, and while embracing him began to beat his chest gently. " What are you doing"? He said. " Why are you beating my chest"?

His wife began wiping the tears from her eyes, and said, "I love you and I love your wonderful thoughtful gift. But why, when I asked for your assistance to clean the kitchen this morning, did your give me such a difficult time? That would have also felt like a wonderful gift to begin my birthday."

*"I think in terms of winning games. I don't look at homeruns. I don't even know if we hit one. But I remember what the score was. A couple of singles here and there and we've won a couple more games."*

**Bobby Cox**

**Manager, Atlanta Braves**

## 2-Errors

Errors in baseball and relationships are costly. One error in a baseball game can end a perfect game. Men understand that in baseball there can be two outs in the ninth inning with the score two runs to zero. The pitcher on the mound has given up no runs up to that point. The next batter the pitcher walks, giving the other team a runner at first.

The next batter hits an ordinary grounder to third base; an easy play to first, to end the game. But instead, the third baseman bobbles the ball in his haste, causing a significant error, now leaving two men on base with one in scoring position. The next batter up hits a homerun on the second pitch, to end the game. The game is over because of one error at the wrong time. That same error made in the third inning, not leading to a run scored, would have had less significance, but in the ninth inning, leading to the loss of the game, it became an error that was deadly.

**Errors can be costly, and sometimes very difficult to overcome.**

In relationships a man's error may never disappear from a woman's heart. Sometimes one error can cause a relationship to fall apart. Other errors will continue to build up in the relationship causing resentment and anger and eventually lead to the relationship ending. Many times men can be hitting singles while not realizing how damaging their errors are in the relationship. And in each relationship women will score errors differently. When you and your partner begin playing baseball together, it is important that you understand what she constitutes as an error and how it weakens the nature of your relationship.

**How one error can be costly even when surrounded by basehits**.

> **Man**: I appreciate you taking my clothes to the cleaners today. Thank you. Dinner was great. You are so wonderful. I enjoyed speaking to you this afternoon on the phone. I'm glad you had a good day. By the way, I just noticed, *WHAT DID YOU DO TO YOUR HAIR?* It looks different. Oh, also I fixed the leaky faucet, and I picked up a movie at Blockbuster, and I spoke to the babysitter about this weekend.
>
> **Partner**: What don't you like about my hair?
> I thought you would love it!

**Certainly each woman may respond differently to this one line, but that is what this book is about. To begin to understand the scorekeeping in the relationship you are in.**

When you make an error, take responsibility and apologize, and strive to become the best fielder you can be, avoiding errors in the future.

# Possible errors in relationships

1-         Failing to hit singles (reread singles)
2-         Criticizing and judging
3-         Lying and cheating
4-         Lacking respect and affection
5-         Making love without feeling intimately connected
6-         Controlling and dominating
7-         Complaining and nagging
8-         Being lazy
9-         Taking the relationship for granted
10-        Lacking romance
11-        Humiliating your partner in public or private
12-        Not listening to what your partner is saying
13-        Not defending your partner's honor
14-        Having expectations

Add other errors- Have your partner share what she may say constitutes an error. And add those.

15-

16-

17-

18-

*" I never understood and still don't understand why the fans are obsessed with them. I think watching a guy hit a ball over the fence and trot around the bases is actually pretty boring."*

**Hank Aaron On Homeruns**

### 3- Homeruns

In baseball, homeruns are always impressive. Everyone wants to hit homeruns.  Yet everyone also knows homeruns can't be hit as often as singles. It is important for men to understand that a homerun is one run. Three singles equal one run. One double and a single are a run. Of course some homeruns occur with runners on base, so that a homerun can be equivalent to more than one run. But men have to remember those men were on base from those non-impressive singles. Women are attracted to men who hit homeruns, but deep meaningful relationships that develop outrageous intimacy still become manifested from the hitting of consistent singles and by avoiding errors. Also remember, homerun hitters tend to strike out more often than other players, since they are always attempting to hit a homerun.

In relationships men also love to hit homeruns. And each man may use a different yardstick to measure what a home run may be. It is important for a man to understand that what he believes is a homerun may be a single or even a strikeout for his partner. Probably more relationships fail because of not understanding the proper scoring of attempted homeruns in relationships.

When a man hits what he believes is a homerun, he always

assumes it is a grand slam with three runners on base. Most men have a difficulty comprehending that their homerun, which they think sailed out of the ballpark, could even be considered in the same breath as three singles. Of course, for his partner, her reply to his homerun can be,

**" I missed it.  Where did you say it went?"  or**

**" You may have seen a homerun, but I saw a swing and a miss for strike three"**

As you are playing baseball with your partner discover what the real homeruns are for her.

## Possible Homeruns in Relationships

1- A romantic letter or postcard sent to your partner for no particular reason, other than sharing your love.

2- Creating a vacation get away where you have taken care of all the arrangements including who is taking care of the children if you have any.

3- A proposal of marriage is a definite home run if the relationship has been evolving in this direction. (This can be a strike out if your proposal is denied.)

4- A planned date, which includes an elegant, romantic dinner, dancing, and entertainment.

5- A poem or song written by yourself and sung to your partner.

6- Intimate listening- learning to hear your partner in such a way that it opens her up to trust you in ways she never could trust anyone else. This also allows her to discover things about herself or rediscover things about herself.

7- A special gift- particularly one that you know your partner would love.

8- A sensuous massage with relaxing music and scented oils, perhaps developing into a beautiful shared evening of tender love and expressed sex.

9- A simple planned evening at a hotel or inn,

where all plans have been made by you, including taking care of the children if you have any.

10- Doing something your partner would love to do, even though you would rather do something else, yet you love being with her and appreciate pleasing her.

11- Planning something different from the ordinary.

**In relationships it is important to create shared experiences that sometimes change the routine.**

12- A candlelight dinner you have prepared yourself, with a bottle of her favorite wine.

13- Remembering special occasions.

14- Making her feel supported, and confident that you will be there in any moment, or any emergency.

15- Observing your partner's needs or desires and taking care of them before she makes a request.

Add your own homeruns to the list and have your partner share, what might be a homerun for her.

16-
17-
18-
19-
20-

**Remember, as wonderful as homeruns are to hit; many attempted homeruns turn into strikeouts.**

A good friend of mine had planned a spectacular evening with his wife. He had front row tickets to a play, backstage passes to meet all the stars, reservations at the finest restaurant, and a luxury limousine hired for the evening. He believed this was going to be a major grand slam, since it was also a surprise.

What he didn't realize was that his wife had worked hard that day, she was exhausted and the last thing she wanted to do was leave her cozy home and go out and interact with people all evening.

His outrageous excitement was met by her annoyance and anger. He felt hurt because all the effort and love he put into creating the evening had been rejected. She felt disrespected and taken for granted that he simply assumed that she would want to go without any earlier notice. When his rejected pain reacted to her disrespected pain, he became upset, rather than understanding. The outcome was that his homerun turned into a strike out. All he truly wanted to do was share his love with his partner, yet sadly, the outcome was just the opposite. At times like these, men need to learn how to turn attempted homeruns into marvelous, daring triples that can bring a relationship to a deeper sense of commitment and intimacy.

Yet when homeruns are hit, particularly grand slams, they can recharge a relationship that has been losing, but without consistent singles it will begin to lose again. Of course, Mark McGuire and Sammy Sosa homeruns can ignite a relationship as well as inspire an evening of wonderful intimate lovemaking. When you break records, relationships open to new levels of romantic intimacy.

*" That homerun was very, very special.  Anytime you win a game it's very, very special."*

**Mark McGuire**

*"I almost cried.  I didn't cry because I'm a tough guy."*

**Sammy Sosa**
**After McGuire's 62nd Homerun**

## 4-  Triples

Triples in baseball are seldom hit, making it one of the most exciting plays in the game to watch. Whereas a homerun's magnificence is portrayed by its power, a triple's uniqueness is manifested by the players speed, agility, instincts, and at times bold daring sense of adventure, as the runner attempts to stretch a double into a triple.

In relationships, when attempted homeruns are rejected, a wonderful opportunity becomes available for soulful triples. Triples occur when you are able to lovingly accept and understand your partner's response toward your attempted homerun. At that moment your partner may feel you are truly listening to her feelings and thoughts, which allows her to totally experience the depth of your commitment and love.

She may feel excited by your willingness to stretch deep within, exploring places in each other's spirits seldom visited.

**Triples can take relationships to new and exciting places.**

Sometimes when you are willing to hit triples, your partner may also begin to stretch, and in that instant your attempted homerun may now sail out of the park.

**Women appreciate men who are willing to stretch deep inside themselves and go for triples.**

### Questions:

1-      How have you responded in the past to rejected homeruns?

2-      How has that affected the relationships you've been in?

3-      Have you turned rejected homeruns into triples?

4-      How did that affect the relationship?

**Have a conversation with your partner about triples and how they can open up your relationship to new and exciting places.**

**5-      Strikeouts**

Strikeouts in baseball are simply failing to get to base. The player had an opportunity to get a hit but instead struck out! As I mentioned, strikeouts occur often when players are attempting to hits homeruns, and most homerun hitters strike out the most. Also, strikeouts can happen at any time in the game, just like errors.

In baseball, a strikeout with two outs and the bases loaded in the ninth inning is more devastating than striking out with no outs and no runners on base in the third inning. Like errors, strikeouts lead to a relationship weakening, and can eventually lead to losing the game.

In the relationship, strikeouts also can occur at any time, and interfere with the romantic intimacy of the relationship. Sometimes, men strike out trying too hard attempting to hit a homerun. Yet other times men strikeout out by not guarding home plate closely enough and simply watching a third called strike whiz by. In relationships it is important to know how your partner calls strikes. And, if you didn't pay attention to her strike zone on the first few pitches, don't expect sympathy on the third strike.

## Possible Strike outs in relationships

1-      Poor communication- If your partner is playing baseball, and you are playing tennis, it will lead to frustrations that weaken the relationship. If you begin having an open intimate conversation with your partner that creates wonderful trust between you both, but then come to a disagreement with one another where she feels your judgment or ridicule, the intimacy will turn into defensive armoring and resentment and anger. Men need to understand that is a big strikeout that could have been a grand slam.

2-      Not keeping your word-  Our word is our bond and when you begin breaking your word the bond of the relationship begins to break. If you said you were going to do something and didn't, that can be a strikeout. It is important to adjust your stance in the batter's box and understand her strike zone.

3-      Changing plans at the last minute- Typically your partner may want to feel that she is part of the decision making process and that you have respected her enough to let her know certain things in advance. Remember, you and your partner are a team!

4-      Making other things more important than the relationship. Many times unknowingly, men will make their careers, other projects, and personal matters more important than their partner. If your partner is the right partner, she will want you taking care of all your other projects, yet, in her heart, she desires to feel that she is a priority in your life.

5-      Poor social habits- Not putting toothpaste cap on toothpaste, not putting food back in the refrigerator, not being neat and clean, not taking responsibility around the house all can be strikeouts.

6-      Having sex without romantic intimacy and falling asleep, not realizing that she is now wound up sexually, and feeling as if she has been used.

7-      Bringing friends home or inviting friends over without first requesting and communicating with your partner. This is even a bigger strikeout if you then expect her to then serve everyone dinner and be the perfect hostess.

8-      Expecting attention and affection after you have had a long day and complaining if your expectation is not manifested.

9-      Complaining and whining about life.

10-     Being cheap- Although your partner will appreciate your abilities to save money and your skill in bargaining, she may feel unloved if the focus of the relationship is on cost containment, rather than romance and abundance.

Add your own strikeouts and have your partner add what she considers strikeouts.

1-

2-

3-

4-

5-

6-

Remember that strikeouts can change in the development of the relationship. When dating, the strike zone may be different than in a committed relationship. And strike zones can change with different partners. In baseball, pitchers and hitters have to adapt quickly to who that umpire is in that given game.

### 6- Batting Average/Pitcher's ERA

Having a good batting average in baseball is everything. The best baseball players typically have excellent batting averages. This means they get on base a good percentage of the time they are up. In baseball, a player who can get three hits for every ten at bats is a superstar worth millions of dollars. Imagine hitting three singles each day in your relationship, and an occasional homerun. How might that affect the overall score of your relationship.

A good batting average simply means that you are a consistent player. This is a baseball player the manager and the rest of the team want up to bat when runs are needed or runners are on base.

In relationships, if you have a good batting average, your partner begins to trust you more, as she sees and believes in your word and behavior. For her, this consistency signifies that you are making her important and sharing your love and affections. This allows her to open further to you, which then can lead to a homerun.

A pitcher's ERA is similar to a batting average. Yet, the goal of the pitcher is to keep the other team from getting hits and scoring runs. An excellent pitcher is also one who is consistent. A good pitcher can throw the ball where he wants to and how he wants to. And, a good pitcher understands the batters he faces and adapts quickly to the strike zone.

The best pitchers have a low ERA, giving up few runs, because of their skill, focus, concentration, and consistency.

A woman wants to be able to depend on her partner and to trust that he will be there to take care of business as well as take care of her. Even the most creative, successful woman wants to feel protected and secure by the consistent strength, wisdom, and guidance of her partner.

Greg Maddux of the Atlanta Braves manifests these qualities. His teammates know when he pitches he is in charge. The team doesn't feel as much pressure to get runs, knowing that when he is on the mound, they are almost certain to win the game.

When a woman is that certain of her partner, a relationship can only improve, for she is experiencing homeruns, singles, and triples being hit daily.

## 7- Wild Pitches

In baseball, a wild pitch thrown by a pitcher can be costly at times and at others times embarrassing and sloppy. Wild pitches simply mean that the pitcher is out of control, and there is a potential for danger. If there are runners on base, runners can advance when there are wild pitches.

In relationships, when men throw wild pitches, it is represented by their being out of control. This can seriously damage relationships. Repeatedly throwing wild pitches will lead to losing a game in baseball and end the game of the relationship.

## Possible wild pitches in relationships

1- Drinking too much alcohol, leading to improper altered behavior.
2- Abusive behavior physical or emotional.
3- Using drugs and manifesting an addictive behavior.
4- Speaking harshly and accusingly.
5- Being demanding.
6- Being unreasonable.
7- Flirting with other women.
8- Not introducing your partner as your girlfriend or significant other at a social gathering.
9- Touching or grabbing her inappropriately at social gatherings.
10- Telling her she needs to lose weight, have a facial, exercise more, eat less, as well as many other things that she will not appreciate.
11- Losing your temper-Insulting her.

**It is important to understand that certain behaviors are unacceptable and a man may need assistance to actually improve. Counseling, spiritual healing, or workshops may be necessary so that wild pitches can be controlled and eventually avoided altogether.**

**All great athletes have great coaches.**

If you throw any wild pitches, be willing to recognize them.

Ask your partner if she feels that you throw wild pitches and be open to discuss this with her, and how you might regain your control so she can feel confident with you on the pitcher's mound again.

## 8- Slumps

In baseball even the best players can get in episodes called slumps. It can be a batter's slump, as well as a pitcher's slump. This is a time when the player can't seem to do anything right. The best hitter is now having a difficult time getting on base or a pitcher is having a difficult time winning a game. Most slumps will end as mysteriously as they began. Managers, coaches, and the other players have to keep their faith in a player when he is in a slump. Many times when a player is in a slump, a coach will specifically work with a player to discover what the problem may be. Though it does not occur too often, a player who was considered a star may remain in a slump too long and the managers may lose faith in his ability to return. When that occurs, the player can be traded or sent down to the minors.

There can be slumps in relationship also. When your partner has faith in you even when you are down, you will feel supported, but if you are down too long your partner may lose faith in you and your natural abilities to return. It is important for couples to endure slumps if their relationship is to evolve and grow into one that is meaningful and lasting. Slumps can occur for various reasons and both partners must continue to be in communication to bring back the abundance and strength into the relationship. When a partner has a slump, it is important to observe your initial evaluations of this player to see her past track record. Many times relationships end during these difficult times. When a couple works through a slump together, they build a stronger foundation, based on trust and integrity.

When you are in a slump it is easy to feel frustrated and confused. It is important to remember that it is the best players who occasionally get into a slump, perhaps because of their expectations of scoring and winning. Babe Ruth, Mickey

Mantle, John Smoltz, Steve Avery, Chipper Jones, and Andrew Jones, have all felt the effects of a slump, so you share good company at those times.

You may feel that you are trying to do everything right, attempting to break out of the slump, and yet you may feel like you are sinking deeper into depression.

Coaches are always learning new ways to assist their players out from their slumps. But there is nothing more important than the player feeling that the team has not lost confidence and faith in his abilities.

*"I am not superman, I am human. Everyone goes through a slump. I just stay really positive about the slump."*

**Andrew Jones**

**Centerfielder for Atlanta Braves**

## Possible reasons for slumps in relationships

1- Loss of job, or did not get promotion
2- Illness
3- Unexpected loss of income
4- Emotional or physical stress unresolved
5- Problems with ex-spouse or children, if they exist in your life
6- Depressed- Lack of vision in your life
7- Frustrations in relationship or career not being resolved

## Exercise to assist your partner who's in a slump

1- Be certain you are willing to be open to listen to your partner's frustrations, and confusions.
2- Be clear how much you have confidence and love for your partner.
3- Feel strong within yourself so that your partner can share with you, without you taking anything personally.
4- Discover a good time for you and your partner to explore this exercise without being interrupted.

Sit across from your partner, while both of you are relaxed. Ask your partner if she is willing to participate in this exercise. If she says yes, then you can begin. If she says no, then lovingly respect her wishes at this time, and let her know you are available for her in any way possible.

**Opening to your partner**.

Name of your partner, I would like for you to share with me, as best you can any frustrations, or confusions you have been feeling. I promise I will listen without reacting to anything you say, unless you want me to respond to you.

Name of partner, I love you, and I have faith and confidence in you and in us, and I believe we can work through any slump together.

**Allow your partner to share.**

Listen with attentiveness and support. Allow the natural rhythm of the sharing to unfold, as your partner authentically trusts that you are listening without judgment. She may even say how different this feels to be able to express herself without feeling criticized or judged.

Occasionally reaffirm your love and support, acknowledging her willingness to be open as she is sharing her frustrations.

Ask your partner if there is anything you can do to assist her, and remind her of your love.

If the conversation becomes more relaxed, begin to share about your mutual visions in life and ways to rediscover the passions and fun again.

Review with each other how to hit singles, and begin to explore how to get in scoring position once again in life.

*Remember the best players fall into slumps.*
*Be patient, keep faith, and express your love.*

Write out your own possible slumps and have your partner write out hers.

1.
2.
3.
4.
5.
6.
7.
8.

### Questions:

1. What have you done to get out of slumps in the past?

2. Have you ever asked for assistance when you have been in a slump?
What was the outcome?

## 9- Sacrifice Bunts

In baseball, managers will sometimes signal a player who is at bat to lay down a sacrifice bunt when there is at least a runner at first base. The strategy of this maneuver is to advance a player who is at first base to scoring position. When the play is executed properly, the runner advances to second base and the batter is typically thrown out at first. Even though the batter is out, he has accomplished his job. Sacrifices in baseball are extremely important for teams to win.

In relationships, sacrifices are essential for partnerships to evolve and fulfill visions that couples want to see manifested in their lives. Sacrifices occur when you want your relationship to develop into meaningful, intimate partnerships that are serving the team to win.

Sometimes partners have difficulty sacrificing for each other, since it may seem as if you are giving something up. If there is no trust between both people, the conversations of sacrifice will be met with resistance and stubbornness.

In baseball, the player who lays down the sacrifice bunt is giving up the possibility of hitting a single or homerun. Certainly a player would become frustrated if he was not committed to the team but instead was simply thinking of himself.

In relationships, sacrificing for your partner and the vision you both share is necessary for relationships to grow, and also allows each person to feel authentic, soulful love from their partner.

It is as if to say, "I am willing to give up something that is important for me, so that the dreams we have for our relationship can be fulfilled. That is how deep my love is for you and my wish for our relationship to grow."

If a partner is willing to make a sacrifice, though does not feel appreciated by the other person, she will begin to feel resentful, disrespected, and used.

**Sacrificing is a sacred gift in relationships that always must be honored and treasured.**

Possible Sacrifice Bunts in Relationships

A. Sacrificing old habits

1- The willingness to give up certain habits if they do not empower the relationship.

a. Excessive drinking, drugs, smoking

2- Giving up a single lifestyle that you were used to that does not serve the team.

a. Going out with friends on a regular basis without your partner.

b. Having friends over to the house without asking your partner.

c. Staying up late at night.

d. Cleanliness habits, in your home, that were ok for you but are not ok for your partner.

B. Sacrifices that require soulful thought and intimate communication.

1- A decision to have a baby and understanding what sacrifices may be necessary.

2- Sacrifices in delaying career opportunities or education goals.

3- One partner supporting another partner through school.

4- A sacrifice of leaving your job to move to another city or state where your partner lives or where your partner has been transferred.

5- The sacrifice of one person working supporting a family, while the other partner is at home raising children.

It is important to know you are a team when making sacrifice bunts that support the vision of the relationship. When your partner feels your willingness to make sacrifices, it will allow her to feel your devoted love, which will deepen the intimacy of the relationship.

Questions:

1- In the past what sacrifice bunts have you laid down in relationships?

2- What sacrifice bunts have partners given to you?

3- In your present relationship what sacrifice bunts have been manifested? Are there any sacrifice bunts that are being explored at the present time?

4- How did your partners or you feel when your sacrifice bunts were not appreciated and respected?

# Relationship Athletics

## Baseball Scoreboard

## Days

| | 1 | 2 |
|---|---|---|
| Homeruns | | |
| Sosa McGuire Style | | |
| Triples | | |
| Errors | | |
| Strikeouts | | |
| Wild Pitches | | |
| Bad Errors | | |
| Bad Strikeouts | | |
| Low Era | | |
| Bad Wild Pitches | | |
| Working Through Slumps | | |
| Not Working Through Slumps | | |
| Sacrifice Bunts | | |
| Single Hits | | |

| | | | | | |
|---|---|---|---|---|---|
| Homerun | 1 | Bad errors | -3 | Bad Wild Pitch | -3 |
| Sosa McGuire Homerun | 4 | Triple | 4 | Sacrifice Bunts | 3 |
| Strikeouts | -1 | Single | 1 | | |
| Errors | -1 | Pitching Low ERA | 4 | | |
| Bad Strikeouts | -3 | Wild Pitch | -1 | | |
| Working Through Slumps | 4 | Not Working Through Slumps | -4 | | |

# Relationship Athletics

## Baseball Scoreboard

## Days

| 3 | 4 | 5 | 6 | 7 |
|---|---|---|---|---|
|   |   |   |   |   |
|   |   |   |   |   |
|   |   |   |   |   |
|   |   |   |   |   |
|   |   |   |   |   |
|   |   |   |   |   |
|   |   |   |   |   |
|   |   |   |   |   |
|   |   |   |   |   |
|   |   |   |   |   |
|   |   |   |   |   |
|   |   |   |   |   |
|   |   |   |   |   |
|   |   |   |   |   |

| | | | | | |
|---|---|---|---|---|---|
| Homerun | 1 | Bad errors | -3 | Bad Wild Pitch | -3 |
| Sosa McGuire Homerun | 4 | Triple | 4 | Sacrifice Bunts | 3 |
| Strikeouts | -1 | Single | 1 | | |
| Errors | -1 | Pitching Low ERA | 4 | | |
| Bad Strikeouts | -3 | Wild Pitch | -1 | | |
| Working Through Slumps | 4 | Not Working Through Slumps | -4 | | |

# Relationship Athletics

## Baseball Scoreboard

## Days

| | 1 | 2 |
|---|---|---|
| Homeruns | | |
| Sosa McGuire Style | | |
| Triples | | |
| Errors | | |
| Strikeouts | | |
| Wild Pitches | | |
| Bad Errors | | |
| Bad Strikeouts | | |
| Low Era | | |
| Bad Wild Pitches | | |
| Working Through Slumps | | |
| Not Working Through Slumps | | |
| Sacrifice Bunts | | |
| Single Hits | | |

| | | | | | |
|---|---|---|---|---|---|
| Homerun | 1 | Bad errors | -3 | Bad Wild Pitch | -3 |
| Sosa McGuire Homerun | 4 | Triple | 4 | Sacrifice Bunts | 3 |
| Strikeouts | -1 | Single | 1 | | |
| Errors | -1 | Pitching Low ERA | 4 | | |
| Bad Strikeouts | -3 | Wild Pitch | -1 | | |
| Working Through Slumps | 4 | Not Working Through Slumps | -4 | | |

# Relationship Athletics

## Baseball Scoreboard

## Days

| 3 | 4 | 5 | 6 | 7 |
|---|---|---|---|---|
|   |   |   |   |   |
|   |   |   |   |   |
|   |   |   |   |   |
|   |   |   |   |   |
|   |   |   |   |   |
|   |   |   |   |   |
|   |   |   |   |   |
|   |   |   |   |   |
|   |   |   |   |   |
|   |   |   |   |   |
|   |   |   |   |   |
|   |   |   |   |   |
|   |   |   |   |   |
|   |   |   |   |   |

| | | | | | |
|---|---|---|---|---|---|
| Homerun | 1 | Bad errors | -3 | Bad Wild Pitch | -3 |
| Sosa McGuire Homerun | 4 | Triple | 4 | Sacrifice Bunts | 3 |
| Strikeouts | -1 | Single | 1 | | |
| Errors | -1 | Pitching Low ERA | 4 | | |
| Bad Strikeouts | -3 | Wild Pitch | -1 | | |
| Working Through Slumps | 4 | Not Working Through Slumps | -4 | | |

"It doesn't happen just in games.  Its starts in practice and that's the way I approach it."

Michael Jordon

# Basketball

"I play the game to win, have fun, and make people happy."

Magic Johnson

|   1   |   2   |   3   |   4   |
|-------|-------|-------|-------|
|       |       |       |       |
|       |       |       |       |

**Basketball**

Basketball has four quarters

1 – Points
2 – Fouls- Fouling out
3 – Assists –Teamwork
4 – Rebounds
5 – Dunks
6 – Foul Shots
7 – Blocked Shots
8 - Jumpballs
9 - Screens

> "He is the most exciting awesome player in the game today. I think its just God disguised as Michael Jordon."

> **Larry Byrd**

## 1- Points

In basketball, points are necessary to win the game. They are similar to the singles in baseball. Though in basketball, players shoot more often than baseball players come to bat. In basketball there is a high percentage of missed shots in comparison to shots made.

Even Michael Jordan, who is the best basketball player ever, can miss half the shots he takes and still score thirty plus points. But in the game of basketball, the key is to continue to take shots. That's how a player improves and increases his confidence and begins to score more points which wins games.

Missing shots in basketball is not like striking out in baseball. As a player authentically attempts to score baskets, the percentage of his point average will usually increase. It is important not to be frustrated when you miss in basketball, for then you may become tentative and refrain from shooting.

In relationships, points are necessary for a relationship to grow and develop. In relationships when you are scoring points, your partner will feel like you are committed to the relationship moving forward. Yet when you miss shots in the process, your partner will still feel connected to you if she feels like you are giving your best and attempting to score points. She doesn't want you to stop shooting. Ideally, she wants to believe in you and see your confidence increase in the relationship.

## Points in Relationships

1. All singles in baseball equal points in basketball
2. Helping around the house with chores and assisting her with outside chores
3. Keeping things organized in the house
4. Buying her a gift for no reason, sending flowers, a card

## Missed Shots in Relationships

1. You prepared dinner, but it did not come out as good as you hoped.
2. Accommodations at an Inn that you reserved for a romantic weekend are not as intimate as you expected.
3. You purchase her a clothing item but the size or style isn't correct.
4. You clean the house, but not exactly how your partner cleans it.

*If certain missed shots persist, your partner may feel that you are not interested in changing, and that can lead to a foul.*

Make a list of points you think you score in your relationship and ask your partner to share what points she would enjoy.

1.
2.
3.
4.
5.

Make a list of missed shots and share them with your partner.

1-

2-

3-

4-

5-


Ask your partner to share with you her feelings regarding your missed shots.

## 2 – Fouls – Fouling Out

In basketball, fouls are costly. They allow the other team to have opportunities to score points; and, if you get too many fouls, you can foul out of the game.

In relationships, fouls are significant for there are only so many fouls you will be allowed before you foul out of the relationship. And, depending upon the type of foul, and how the partner you're with keeps score, you may be in a relationship that has ended months, or years before you realize it.

It is important to know when you have committed a foul and what fouls are in the relationship. Once you understand what your partner has determined is a foul, then it's important to not execute that same foul again, as well as other fouls. Even if you are scoring lots of points and getting lots of assists and rebounds, you can still foul out of the relationship.

Fouls in relationships are actions and/or attitudes that are not tolerated for too long. And for each woman the scoring of fouls will be different. You may have no idea you have fouled out of the game or how many fouls you have, if you do not understand your partner's scoring system.

This is an area where many relationships fail, when men tend to not listen attentively to their partner's <u>requests</u>, <u>concerns</u>, and <u>desires</u>. Men, often in their stubbornness, resistance, and desire to be right, break down the connection of love, compassion and romantic feelings in the relationship. A woman may begin to feel powerless and hopeless and see ending the relationship as the only possibility when the fouls continue.

Fouls that lead to fouling out of a relationship can be classified in two categories; offensive fouls and defensive fouls. Men who foul in the first category usually understand why they foul out of the game and why the relationship is over. Men who foul in the second category tend to be more oblivious to the fouls that they make. They may feel that they have been scoring points and expressing love and tenderness in the relationship, and truly can find themselves surprised when they are told the game is over and they have fouled out. They may believe they were about to shoot for an outside three-point play but the clock ran out.

## Possible Fouls in Relationships

A – Offensive Fouls

1- Talking nasty to your partner in public or private
2- Cheating or lying
3- Emotional or physical abuse
4- Flirting with other women in front of your partner
5- Judging and criticizing your partner and telling her what she should do to get better, or look better.
6- Alcohol or drug abuse
7- Lacking respect

B – Defensive Fouls

1- Wanting to watch television even after your partner has requested wanting to share something with you .

2- Your partner requesting something, yet your reply is " I don't do it that way."
   a- Folding clothes a certain way.
   b- Putting dishes in dishwasher a certain way.
   c- Putting things away after using them.
   d- Wanting to go somewhere, yet you would rather stay home.
   e- Buying certain brands of food, yet you purchase other brands.
3- Forgetting when your partner has made certain requests
4- Arguing over differences of opinion, rather than respecting your partner's opinion
5- Putting things off, after promises have been made. It seems like something will get done, but when?

Make a list of your own fouls, and have your partner share what might be offensive or defensive fouls to her.

1.
2.
3.
4.
5.

*"I think we both sense if one us is going well, we continue to let that person go at it until it's time for the other one to step up. We do it naturally. We know each other so well, it's just instinct."*

**Scottie Pippen**
**Referring to Michael Jordon**
**And himself**

### 3- Assists

In basketball assists occur when a player makes a key pass to another player who scores the points. Some of the best basketball players are noted more for their assists than for their own scoring ability. And, typically, the best players in the game, besides being great scorers, are great at assists.

Probably anyone who has seen Magic Johnson play, or Larry Bird, knows how important and effective assists are in the game of basketball. Also, assists can be a wonderful, creative and artistic expression of the player at the top of his game. Though scoring points wins games in basketball, assists act as the matrix that connects a team, aiding it in functioning as a whole unit, where each player is as important as the other.

Like the spokes on a wheel, or legs on a chair, each is necessary for the ultimate creative balance and maximum performance; and so it is for a team.

Phil Jackson, the successful coach of the Chicago Bulls, explained in his book "Sacred Hoops" how he approached Michael Jordon, the best basketball player ever. At the time Jordon was scoring forty points a game, sometimes fifty and even sixty points in a game. Yet somehow, the team might still lose. The Bulls had not yet won a championship, and for Jordon, that was the next hurdle. Jackson, who had been a student of

Zen philosophy, simply asked Jordon if he would be willing to score fewer points and have the team win more games. Jordon's simple reply was "show me". Sometimes in relationships men walk around "strutting their stuff" like proud lions, as if to say, "Look at me, I'm great". Women will be drawn to men who score lots of points, and who are powerful players, though if women are not feeling <u>assists</u> and not feeling acknowledged, they will begin to either wither in the relationship or become angry, retreating emotionally and physically from the relationship. At that time, they may begin looking for other high scorers, who like to pass better, or hopefully, they may decide to communicate their upsets to you. If your partner does communicate to you, be certain to assist her by listening supportively and lovingly. For that will be an assist that scores points.

Relationships are always empowered by assists, and this behavior in the relationship may take the form of unselfish acts. These expressions in the relationship can be manifested by serving, sharing, and helping your partner, and are received as precious gifts. Many times these unselfish acts can be subtle, and receive no glory, just like an assist in a basketball game, allowing the other person to score the basket, who then feels the appreciation from the crowd. A relationship, like a team, is meant to function as a whole where each player grows and becomes better, and where one player does not overshadow the other.

I'm certain Jordon felt he was doing his best, playing his heart out, scoring points, though not fully understanding that he was intimidating and disempowering the other players.

In relationships, men can feel like they are doing their best, working hard, trying to please their partner, yet not realizing when their partner is feeling intimidated rather than supported. Your partner may feel that her job, her dreams, and her life are not respected and admired like yours if she is not receiving your generous assistance and understanding.

Jackson proved to Jordon that by engaging the other players more in the game, they began to feel more comfortable playing with the greatest player in the world. Then they became more confident and didn't feel like they failed if they missed a shot. The players on the team began to realize that their contributions were as important as Jordan's was for the team to win. Since changing to this Zen type approach the Bulls have won more championships than any other basketball team.

Jordon still continued to score, but now he was even more effective, since, when he had the ball he could choose to score, or create an assist and give other players the spotlight.

*REMEMBER,   ASSITS   IN   RELATIONSHIPS   SCORE POINTS IN RELATIONSHIPS!!!!*

## ASSISTS THAT EMPOWER RELATIONSHIPS

A-Unselfish Acts

1-  Anytime you do something your partner would like to do; though it is not your favorite choice, that constitutes an unselfish act. She may love the ballet and you love going to basketball games. Going with her and enjoying being with her and her appreciation of the ballet scores points, by the nature of your generous spirit.

The message you are sending her is, " I enjoy being with you anywhere you are, and I love doing things that bring you joy."

If unselfish acts are manifested into a complaint or expectation, then they are not truly unselfish acts, and they will not score points.  Instead, they can turn into fouls.

<u>Example:</u> If you go to the ballet with your partner, then complain during the performance, or you say " I'll go with you to the ballet this week, if you go with me to a basketball game next week."

2- You have something fixed you know your partner was having difficulties with: her car, washing machine, squeaky chair, dryer, leaky faucet.

3- Going to a party with your partner, even when you would rather stay home, or staying home when you would rather go to the party.

4- Asking her what she would enjoy doing, and doing it. Where she would enjoy going, and going there.

5- Have love-making be the most generous act, bathing your partner with love and sensuous pleasure. Give to your partner totally, until she is filled with your love.


*Unselfish acts always have you thinking of your partner's needs and desires as an expression of your love.*

B- Sharing, Serving, Helping Assists

1- Sharing your thoughts and affection physically and verbally.

2- Empowering your partner by letting her know how much you love and appreciate her, and how much she contributes to your life, making life that much more wonderful and enjoyable for you.

3- Letting her know how much you want to contribute to her life, bringing out the best in her, so that all her dreams can be fulfilled.

4- The willingness to assist with all the family and children responsibilities, and many of the small things that occur in a household day by day, that many times men are oblivious to.

Helping with little things, and chores around the house may not look like big super star behavior, but they are the assists that score points in the relationship.

5- If your partner is not feeling well, be willing to take care of all her needs. Offer to cook for her, clean the house, buy the groceries, go to the cleaners, and whatever else is necessary to do.

6- Give her a full body massage with soft music and candlelight, allowing her to relax and simply feel your loving attention and affections.

7- Listening with respect and open heart .

Listening to her needs, desires, feelings, upsets, joys, frustrations with undivided attention and respect, while not trying to fix any of her problems, simply allowing her to share herself with you, so that she knows that her communication is important to you.

**" If I can throw a sweet pass, that's better than anything. It's like getting a jumper and a dunk. You advance in three categories. You've made yourself feel good, made that player feel good, and the team scored."**

**Stephen Marbury**

**Basketball Player**

What assists can you begin manifesting in your relationship?

1-

2-
3-
4-
5-
6-
7-
8-
9-
10-


What assists did you resist in past relationships?

Also practice saying these words during the day to your partner

"How can I assist you?"

Listen closely, then follow through with her requests.

## 4- DUNKS

In basketball, dunks get a lot of attention. When successfully done they score points, though not more than other shots. They are power plays that are aggressive and forceful making a statement.

In relationships, dunks can be impressive and attractive. However, if you don't score points from all angles of the court, and make assists, dunks can lead to a deteriorating relationship fast.

In relationships dunks can resemble an impressive outside appearance without the substance that fills the relationship and has it grow and develop.

Women will initially be drawn to men who can dunk, but if that is all there is, they will soon say good-bye or, sorry, the game is over!

## Dunks in Relationships

1- Men who are loud, and aggressive in public, who get lots of attention. These men are flamboyant and attractive. Women want to be around men who can dunk.

2- Typically men who dunk attract many women to them, though in relationships dunkers can be abusive, controlling and domineering.

3- Women will look at other women who are with dunkers, thinking how lucky they are, while the woman with the dunker may be looking for her exit out of the relationship.

Make a list of Dunks in relationships
1-
2-
3-
4-
5-


*If you enjoy dunking, be certain to improve the rest of your game.*


## 5- FOUL SHOTS

In terms of the style of the shot, foul shots are the opposite of dunks. There is nothing fancy about a foul shot, yet sinking foul shots in a basketball game is essential for winning games. We anticipate basketball players making their foul shots. After all, they are the best in the world. Most of us find it surprising when players miss these shots. It is especially unusual for a player's percentage of foul shots made to be less than sixty percent. For the pros, eight of ten, or eighty percent is considered good.

The reason why we expect foul shots to be made is because anyone who has played basketball can make foul shots.

When I was thirteen years old I won a foul-shooting contest in my age group. I sank eighteen out of twenty shots. Amazingly, that is as good as any pro.

In relationships, foul shots translate into the steady, expected qualities that are important for you to bring into the relationship.

Most of us are surprised when we see two people together for awhile if these qualities do not exist. If foul shots are not being made a high percentage of the time, a relationship is certain to deteriorate. If a couple remains together when anticipated foul shots are not scored, chances are the relationship is held together for the wrong reasons. A woman may be with a dunker, who sure looks good, yet he can't make a foul shot. He's driving his Porsche and everyone you know wishes they were you. She is hoping he'll learn to hit some more foul shots if she is with him long enough. But what if he's not a foul shooter, he's a dunker!

# EXPECTED FOUL SHOTS THAT ARE NECESSARY IN RELATIONSHIPS

### 1- Respect and appreciation

Speaking and communicating with respect to one another and appreciating the other person's qualities and ideas in private and public.

### 2- Trust

Trust is necessary for a relationship to grow. If there isn't trust, because of specific reasons, or suspected reasons, then a relationship will continue to lose. It sometimes is important to seek counseling or workshops to evolve through areas of distrust to regain an honoring of each other's actions and words.

### 3- Generosity and sharing

In relationships, we all want to feel like we are the most important person in our partner's life. Generosity is manifested in many ways in the relationship. You can show generosity through freely speaking loving words, being readily available to listen or to talk, or to spend time as a family unit as well as being generous with money or gifts. When we trust and respect each other generosity naturally flows.

### 4- Assistance and support

We anticipate that in a relationship there will be mutual support and assistance. This can be manifested in the areas of career, family, chores, times of difficulties, child rearing, finances, goals and visions, and spiritual evolving.

## 5- Attraction and love

We expect partners to be attracted to one another in various ways. The attractions can be multifaceted on physical, emotional, and spiritual levels. Simply, attraction has you feel good about your partner. If someone asked you why you were attracted to your partner, you would have specific reasons.

Examples:

1- I think she is beautiful.
2- I think she is smart, wise, intelligent.
3- I like how she communicates her feelings and thoughts.
4- I like how she takes care of herself.
5- I like her self-confidence.
6- I like her body, and I think she is sexy and compassionate.
7- I like how she makes me feel.
8- She's a great cook.
9- She's a great mom.
10- I like her value system of integrity and trust.
11- I like her commitment to her spiritual growth and learning.
12- I like her openness and tenderness.
13- I like her positive attitude.
14- I like her willingness to explore the mystery of our relationship always seeking for it to improve.
15- She's a great artist, healer, athlete.
16- We share similar visions and goals in life.
17- It is so exciting to be with her.

Add your own list and share these verbally with each other.

18-

19-

20-

21-

## 6- VISION

We anticipate partners having similar visions in relationships. This is part of the attraction. Spiritual, emotional, family, career, and wellness are important visions for couples to share. If you are someone who is committed to excellence in your life, we anticipate you're with a partner with similar visions. If you want children, and with someone who doesn't, this is not a shared vision. This can lead to resentment, lack of support, distrust, and a loss of attraction, particularly if a compromise is not agreed upon.

## 7- COMMITMENT

We anticipate partners who have been together for awhile to share commitment with each other. The inner commitment is the bond that holds the relationship together regardless of unforeseen circumstances. It is this bond that never allows a disagreement to be too serious , or a loss of hair, or loss of a job to mean there is loss of a relationship. True commitments in relationships generate the strength and courage to face any obstacles in life and to explore the depth of love physically, emotionally and spiritually in the most precious way.

When all these foul shots are being scored, all of these qualities lead to the noblest forms of love between two people. Love is more than a spoken word, it is anticipating a high percentage of foul shots on a consistent basis.

## 6- REBOUNDS

In basketball, there are offensive and defensive rebounds. The most famous and best rebounder in basketball is Dennis Rodman. Like him or not, he has mastered the art and skill of rebounding. Rebounds are absolutely necessary to win games. Getting rebounds creates the opportunities for points to be scored, and assists to be made. Rebounds occur when there is an attempted shot that is missed, allowing a rebound to occur that creates a new possibility, a new play, a new set up, and a new possible score.

In relationships rebounds are very significant. Relationships can be lost forever, if rebounds are not made when needed. Sometimes rebounds can bring healing to a relationship, as a new play is created between both people.

When there are ongoing missed shots, and fouls without manifesting rebounds, a relationship can begin to lose its spark and its integrity.

Rebounds in relationships relate to healing and growing through pain or difficulties or loss of love. If rebounds occur that lead to assists, and points, then couples have the opportunity to get back what was lost and discover new heightened possibilities to bring into the relationship.


**Rebounds are necessary to win games.**

## REBOUNDS IN RELATIONSHIPS

1- Where distrust and broken vows have occurred, the rebound is to seek assistance so that the couple can discover the underlying cause of the problems and find new committed vows and renewed passion and trust.

2- Rebounds are necessary after any foul. Defensive

fouls which occur from poor communication, disrespect, and lack of support, can all be transformed when there is a rebound and significant heart-to-heart communication that brings the couple back to their vision and support for one another.

Rebounds always take the form of men taking responsibility and choosing decisions that empower the relationship. When men rebound, it is important to learn to say, "I'm sorry I hurt you, how can I make it up to you, or assist you, for I do want us to win the game.

Rebounds offer opportunities for offensive fouls to be transformed. When two people are committed to changing, and seeking assistance, possibilities of healing can occur where there has been distrust, and pain. However, some offensive fouls don't deserve a rebound to occur, for once you foul out, the game is over, and you're out.

Rebounds, though, represent the possibility for more chances to score and ultimately win the game, allowing couples to learn more about each other and develop strong meaningful relationships. No relationship is ever going to be perfect, but it is the willingness to rebound missed shots and to discover new ways of sharing with each other that will deepen intimacy and love.

Make a list of rebounds that have occurred in your relationships.

1-

2-

3-

4-

5-

6-

7-

8-

Can you see where you didn't rebound efficiently in past relationships?

What have you learned about yourself from rebounding?

## 7- BLOCKED SHOTS

In basketball, blocked shots are necessary to keep the other team from scoring. They are a defensive play in the game, and sometimes-blocked shots can lead to a foul if executed too aggressively.

In relationships, blocked shots can keep a partner from scoring, as well. They manifest as the defensiveness and protection we bring into a relationship, often caused by the fear or hurt; disappointment, or pain that have been internalized from past relationships.

You may be giving your partner authentic affection, yet she is not ready to receive your tenderness. Your partner may feel vulnerable and afraid to let love back into her heart. She may feel uncertain if she can trust someone again; for the last time she was deeply hurt.

Blocked shots sabotage relationships. Relationships are difficult as it is, but with blocked shots existing, it becomes more complicated to achieve healthy communication. Patience, tenderness, understanding, and loving support are important when your partner has these defensive feelings that seem necessary to her. Counseling and workshops may be helpful to assist partners through these areas so that the relationship can score points and win the game.

It is important for couples to be willing to explore their blocked shots, so that an intimate relationship of trust does occur.

## BLOCKED SHOTS IN RELATIONSHIPS

1- Fears
2- Unwillingness to look at past hurts
3- Controlling, dominating behavior
4- Running away when faced with problems in the relationship
5- Victim type behavior
6- Manipulative behavior
7- Inability to express emotions and feelings
8- Unwarranted anger and resentment
9- Defensiveness


Add to the list of blocked shots

10-
11-
12-
13-


Questions:
1- What blocked shots do you have that interfere with intimate relationships?
2- Can you share your blocked shots with your partner?
3- What are you willing to do to heal blocked shots?


Example:

Workshops, counseling, coaching.

Ask your partner what blocked shots she feels she has.
Can she share her blocked shots with you?

## 8- JUMP BALL

In basketball, jump balls determine who receives possession of the ball. This occurs during confrontations, or beginning the game and starting the second half of the game. It is simply a way to see who gets the ball when no foul has been committed. Jump balls can occur anytime during the game, which makes the outcome of the jump ball more important at crucial times.

In relationships, jump balls are decisions made during the course of the relationship. They can occur on first dates, or in romantic intimate partnerships, and throughout marriage.

Decisions can be as simple as determining at what restaurant to eat, or as complex as deciding to sell your home or move to a different state.

Some jump ball decisions can be agreed upon as easily as flipping a coin, where other decisions can strain a relationship, particularly when it is difficult to discover a compromise or a mutual understanding.

Typically, these decisions are not detrimental to a relationship but if the decision process seems unfair to your partner, it can cause resentment and anger.

There are many decisions that occur continuously throughout every relationship almost telephathically, so it seems.

For instance:

1- Who prepares dinner
2- Who picks up groceries
3- Who pays the bills
4- Who cleans the house
5- Who washes the dishes and loads the dishwasher
6- Who walks the dog
7- Who wakes the children, who reads them a story at

night, who checks their homework

8- Who decides where to go on vacation, when to take a vacation

9- Who picks up the bill on the first date

10- Who will call for a second date

11- Who mows the lawn

**Discover what other telepathic decisions you have made in your relationship or that you made in the past. How did these decisions occur and how did they effect the relationship?**

Question

1- Were the decisions based on a mutual agreement, or compromise, or did someone just decide to make a decision because the other person didn't?

**Example:** If you clean the house, was it based on a mutual agreement or did you clean the house one-day and telepathically got the job.

When partners make decisions based on mutual respect and compromise, the relationship develops further trust and intimacy. If your partner feels like you are making decisions that effect the relationship without her input, she may feel resentful and disrespected. When partners learn how to make decisions together, relying on each other's thoughts and feelings and open discussions, then powerful, dynamic, healthy relationships are possible. More problems occur in relationships because of couples' inability to discuss decisions in a positive manner.

*Anyone who has watched youngsters play basketball will observe how they fight for possession of the ball until a whistle is blown to instigate a jump ball.*

## How to make positive healthy jump ball decisions

1- Create a time where you and your partner are relaxed and without interruptions.
2- Discuss possible strategies in determining choices you make.
3- Discover where compromises are beneficial for empowering your relationship.
4- Discover where one or both of you are being resistant or defensive when communicating about decisions, and determine what decisions will serve the higher goals of the relationship.
5- Gently touch each other, holding each other's hands and verbally appreciate your partner and her willingness to share her thoughts and feelings with you.
6- When faced with difficult decisions, keep the conversation open for discussion allowing each of you to pray and meditate separately, asking for God's assistance. Keep on communicating until a decision that empowers the vision of the relationship is supported by each of you.

## Questions to be shared with your partner:

1- What decisions in your past relationships have you made that didn't serve the best interest of the relationship?
2- How would you face these decisions differently at the present time?
3- What decisions are manifesting in your present relationship?

4- How are you responding to difficult decisions?
5- How are compromises and mutual agreements manifesting in your present relationship?

Always remember in each decision that you and your partner are making, your desire is for the team to win!

*Too often relationships become contests battling for the ball, with each person feeling he or she is doing more than the other person, hoping someone will blow a whistle and call for a jump ball decision.*

What decisions based on compromise have you made in relationships?
1-
2-
3-
4-
5-

What mutual agreement decisions have you made in your relationships?
1-
2-
3-
4-
5-

When decisions are reached in healthy ways each player feels responsible and positive about the choices that are made. Each partner feels like agreements have been made with mutual respect and understanding, and a desire for each person to be the best player he or she can be.

## 9- Screen

In basketball a screen protects a player and allows the player with the ball to create many options in his attempt to assist or score.

In relationships, a screen can be seen as the noble qualities you project when protecting and honoring your partner. In themselves screens do not win basketball games, nor do relationships succeed or fail based on this quality alone. Yet the sense of protecting, defending, and honoring are qualities that women have internalized and desired since the beginning of time.

Even though your partner may not need your protection, she may still long to feel that she is a princess for the right prince.

Regardless of how successful or emotionally strong a woman may be, she will feel as if something is missing when you are not there to defend her honor. Your partner may harbor resentment and feel betrayed by you if you are not willing to stand in her defense. You may be scoring points, connecting with assists, and winning games, yet the partnership itself, will never to get to the NBA Finals.

Though your partner may say that your screen is not necessary, in her heart and soul, she will desire to know that you are courageously and generously willing to be there instantaneously, like a prince gallantly appearing before his princess.

On the basketball court, a player may be running a play toward the basket only to find himself blocked by the opposing team, interfering with the possible scoring of points.

His response to his teammate may be, "How come you didn't give me a screen?"

His teammate may reply, " I thought you had it, all by yourself."

Or " I forgot."

In a relationship, the noble quality of a screen may be more subtle.

These days a woman may feel that she shouldn't expect her partner screening for her. After all, she is successful and powerful and can defend herself. Yet the way to create a championship team is to learn how to support and honor each other, even when it appears it may not be necessary.

**Even when it may seem your partner does not need your screens, always be available to be there.**

<u>Questions:</u>

1- If someone were speaking unkindly about your partner, what would your response be?

2- Do you feel comfortable or uncomfortable defending or protecting or honoring your partner in front of other people?

3- In your past relationships, do you remember at times screening for your partner? What was the outcome? What was the outcome if you didn't screen?

**A Fable**

One day a beautiful Princess was in love with a handsome Prince. The Prince loved to honor and protect his Princess and often risked his life gladly slaying dangerous and treacherous dragons that threatened her kingdom. The Princess was so deeply moved by the Prince's courage and devotion that her heart and spirit felt a love that captured her entire soul.

But as years passed and times began to change, the Princess realized that she, too, could protect and even defend herself courageously against the dragons of the day. But instead of this being a joyous time, it was a time of sadness and confusion for the Prince and Princess. The Princess tried to explain to her Prince that even though she now could defend herself, she still so much desired and needed to feel his honor, respect, strength as well as his unwavering love that had filled her heart in the past. And as she explained, she felt her soul would die without it.

The Prince, though, was still confused, feeling that the Princess no longer needed the very essence of his soul that he longed to give to her. For the Prince, honoring the Princess was as necessary to his life as breathing. He felt that if he could not protect her and show his respect for her in the ways he had always known, that his soul would live no longer. For his true purpose in life was to be her Prince forever.

Well, thankfully, about this time a relationship workshop was scheduled in one of the nearby villages, so after thoughtful reflection they decided to attend.

Amazingly, what they explored was how he could still be a Prince and she could still be a Princess. Once again his spirit felt the richness of being alive, and once again she felt a love that captured and filled her soul.

This is what they discovered!

They learned that, at times the Prince could slay dragons for the Princess, and that at other times, she could slay her own dragons. Even more enlightening was discovering that they could slay dragons together, and at certain times, the Prince could even allow his Princess to slay dragons for him. And most important when they weren't slaying dragons, they could have fun, and laugh, and take walks, and share intimate conversations that empowered the passion and romance of their relationship. And so together, the Prince and Princess lived happily ever after, fully expressed in who they were forever and ever and ever more.

Of course this is only a fable, but share it with your Prince or Princess and observe where there are assists, screens, jump balls, foul shots, points and rebounds manifested throughout the story that awaken the essence of the soul nature of each of us.

# Relationship Athletics

## Basketball Scoreboard

### Days

| | 1 | 2 |
|---|---|---|
| Jump Ball | | |
| Not Good Jump Ball | | |
| Points | | |
| Rebounds | | |
| Assists | | |
| Offence Fouls | | |
| Defense Fouls | | |
| Blocked Shots | | |
| Foul Shots | | |
| Fouls Shots Not Good | | |
| Dunks | | |
| Dunks Not Good | | |
| Screen | | |
| | | |

| | | | | | |
|---|---|---|---|---|---|
| Jump Ball | 3 | Offensive Fouls | -3 | Dunks Not Good | -2 |
| Not Good Jump Ball | -2 | Blocked Shots | -2 | Defensive Fouls | -2 |
| Points | 3 | Foul Shots | 3 | Screen | 2 |
| Rebounds | 2 | Not Good Foul Shots | -3 | No Screen | -2 |
| Assists | 3 | Dunks Good | 2 | | |

# Relationship Athletics

## Basketball Scoreboard

## Days

| 3 | 4 | 5 | 6 | 7 |
|---|---|---|---|---|
|   |   |   |   |   |
|   |   |   |   |   |
|   |   |   |   |   |
|   |   |   |   |   |
|   |   |   |   |   |
|   |   |   |   |   |
|   |   |   |   |   |
|   |   |   |   |   |
|   |   |   |   |   |
|   |   |   |   |   |
|   |   |   |   |   |
|   |   |   |   |   |
|   |   |   |   |   |
|   |   |   |   |   |

| | | | | | |
|---|---|---|---|---|---|
| Jump Ball | 3 | Offensive Fouls | -3 | Dunks Not Good | -2 |
| Not Good Jump Ball | -2 | Blocked Shots | -2 | Defensive Fouls | -2 |
| Points | 3 | Foul Shots | 3 | Screen | 2 |
| Rebounds | 2 | Not Good Foul Shots | -3 | No Screen | -2 |
| Assists | 3 | Dunks Good | 2 | | |

# Relationship Athletics

## Basketball Scoreboard

### Days

| | 1 | 2 |
|---|---|---|
| Jump Ball | | |
| Not Good Jump Ball | | |
| Points | | |
| Rebounds | | |
| Assists | | |
| Offence Fouls | | |
| Defense Fouls | | |
| Blocked Shots | | |
| Foul Shots | | |
| Fouls Shots Not Good | | |
| Dunks | | |
| Dunks Not Good | | |
| Screen | | |
| | | |

| | | | | | |
|---|---|---|---|---|---|
| Jump Ball | 3 | Offensive Fouls | -3 | Dunks Not Good | -2 |
| Not Good Jump Ball | -2 | Blocked Shots | -2 | Defensive Fouls | -2 |
| Points | 3 | Foul Shots | 3 | Screen | 2 |
| Rebounds | 2 | Not Good Foul Shots | -3 | No Screen | -2 |
| Assists | 3 | Dunks Good | 2 | | |

# Relationship Athletics

## Basketball Scoreboard

## Days

| 3 | 4 | 5 | 6 | 7 |
|---|---|---|---|---|
|   |   |   |   |   |
|   |   |   |   |   |
|   |   |   |   |   |
|   |   |   |   |   |
|   |   |   |   |   |
|   |   |   |   |   |
|   |   |   |   |   |
|   |   |   |   |   |
|   |   |   |   |   |
|   |   |   |   |   |
|   |   |   |   |   |
|   |   |   |   |   |
|   |   |   |   |   |
|   |   |   |   |   |
|   |   |   |   |   |

| | | | | | |
|---|---|---|---|---|---|
| Jump Ball | 3 | Offensive Fouls | -3 | Dunks Not Good | -2 |
| Not Good Jump Ball | -2 | Blocked Shots | -2 | Defensive Fouls | -2 |
| Points | 3 | Foul Shots | 3 | Screen | 2 |
| Rebounds | 2 | Not Good Foul Shots | -3 | No Screen | -2 |
| Assists | 3 | Dunks Good | 2 | | |

" I think last year I made a couple of mistakes, and I went for too much instead of playing a little safe...It's just learning how to play golf"

Tiger Woods

# Golf

Par

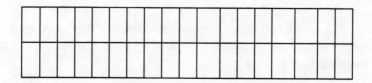

| 1 | 2 | 3 | 4 | 5 | 6 | 7 | 8 | 9 | 10 | 11 | 12 | 13 | 14 | 15 | 16 | 17 | 18 |
|---|---|---|---|---|---|---|---|---|----|----|----|----|----|----|----|----|----|
|   |   |   |   |   |   |   |   |   |    |    |    |    |    |    |    |    |    |
|   |   |   |   |   |   |   |   |   |    |    |    |    |    |    |    |    |    |

**GOLF**

**"The golf ball sitting on the ground doesn't know how old you are"**

> **Mark O' Meara**
>
> **Winner of Masters and British Open 1998**

1- Hole in One

2- From the Tee

3-From the Fairway

4-From the  Rough

5-From the Woods

6-Sand Traps and Water Hazards

7-On the Green and in the Hole

8-Reading the Green

### 1-Hole in One

A hole in one in golf occurs rarely, even with the pros, though it certainly is a fantasy for anyone who swings a golf club.

But a hole in one is a flight of fantasy at best, a shot that will be spoken about for the rest of your life, while you wonder if it magically can ever happen again.

In golf, holes in one typically do not win tournaments, though they certainly create excitement that can turn around someone's game. But anyone who has played golf knows and understands, a hole in one is no guarantee of what the next shot will bring.

Of course if you lose the match and your score is terrible, you can always reflect on that one hole in one that will always bring a smile to your face, even though the spotlight of glory was so short lived.

In relationships, holes in one are all the fantasies you have dreamed about and the fantasies that have occurred. We love to talk about our fantasies and share them with other people, even when some fantasies should be kept private.

In relationships, fantasies can be different for different people, and when these fantasies somehow occur in your life they should be received as wonderful blessings that have manifested. They may be felt as a precious gift, or a new hope, a restored faith, an extraordinary event, or an awakening, as well as a dream or vision materializing in your life.

Sometimes when people meet it can manifest as a hole in one, as if destiny and fate have lent a hand connecting these two souls with each other. It may seem like a miracle has taken place, whereas a moment ago the possibility of these potential lovers did not exist.

Holes in one do not occur on a regular basis, so that when

they do occur in your life, know that this magic will last only so long. The rest of your game has to be consistently improving to have your game last forever.

If your other shots are off, your hole in one fantasy will be a wonderful story that remains in your heart, as a long lost memory.

## **Possible Holes in One in Relationships That are Miraculous**

1- Anytime a relationship may be over and you truly discover how much you care for that person, you can create the possibility of a magical hole in one if the relationship can be turned back on.

2- A romantic passionate encounter that becomes an intimate relationship.

3- Reconnecting with past relationships that are reestablished into new, wonderful friendships after time has gone by.

4- Couples who are in the process of divorce, yet while in the process of healing discover a forgiving heart and a deeper connection with their love.

5- Any illness that is transformed into wellness from a healing recovery that awakens the blessings of being alive.

6- Saying " will you marry me", and the answer simply being "yes".

7-        Watching the birth of your child.

## **Possible Holes in One in Relationships that are Fantasies**

Have fun writing down your Fantasies / Share them with your Partner.

1-
2-
3-
4-
5-
6-
7-
8-
9-
10-


Have your partner share hole in one fantasies with you.

1-
2-
3-
4-
5-


## **2- FROM THE TEE**

In golf, concentration and consistency are absolutely necessary to win tournaments. From the tee, a player must develop a clear vision of where the hole is and a vision of where he wants his ball to land.

From the tee is when a player is playing the first shot, anticipating landing in the fairway or on the green. From the tee sets the tone for the rest of the shots to come.

Vision is essential in the beginning of an intimate relationship. Vision brings forth goals and shared dreams for each partner to empower the other.

Vision is what leads to long lasting romantic relationships where both partners are playing the game of life with the same focus.

A vision is necessary to begin relationships, and visions need to be renewed, reinvented, and communicated on a regular basis so that both partners are playing the game with the same enthusiasm, joy, commitment and love.

### Visions in Relationships

1-    Career Visions
2-    Family Visions
3-    Home Visions
4-    Travel Visions
5-    Education Visions
6-    Health and Wellness Visions
7-    Spiritual Visions
8-    Marriage Visions
9-    Relationship Visions
10-   Children Visions
11-   Personal growth Visions
12-   Dating Visions

Evaluate your visions with your partner and discuss what your visions are and what shared visions you have.

Questions:

1-What specific steps are you taking to fulfill these visions?

2-What are your concerns, doubts, or fears in manifesting your visions?

3-Does your belief system support you fulfilling your visions?

4-Are you having fun creating these visions in your life?

5-Reflecting on your past, what visions have you manifested that you are proud of?

## Vision Exercise

Create a time for yourself when you can relax for at least ten minutes without any interruptions.

1- Close your eyes while either sitting comfortably or lying down. Breathe deeply in through your nose filling your lungs with life, holding it in and expanding your chest for five seconds, then breathe gently out, releasing all tension, anxiety, any tightness in your muscles, any emotional stress, fears, or doubts, of any kind. Allow yourself to continue with this breathing pattern for about two minutes or until you feel a surrendering and a calm peacefulness.

2- Imagine in this feeling of tranquility that it is two years in the future and all your visions are being manifested. You are in the relationship of your dreams. It is filled with joy and passion, laughter and love, and a sacred connectedness that honors your soul. You are living in a beautiful home that reflects your spirit and creativity. Your career is fulfilling, and each day you look forward to waking up and feeling the blessings of being alive. You look forward to bringing your creations into the world and assisting others with your many talents. Your health is excellent, vibrating at a high level of energy. You are strong, radiating light and love in your life and you feel ageless in a body that allows you to enjoy playing each day in your life. Your life is filled with abundance and each day continues to bring more excitement, as you are growing and evolving, opening up to the mysteries of your beingness. You are a witness to your own soul as if it is a mirror of the universe waiting to be explored.

*You feel Great to be alive!*

3- In your vision now look backward in time and clearly see how these manifestations have occurred. See what you have been thinking, doing, and learning. See what commitments you made in your life toward achieving these wonderful successes. See the decisions you made knowing clearly that you deserve life to be filled with your visions being realized. Discover in your visions what specific steps you will begin to take to actualize these gifts into your life.

Each day meditate into your vision so that it becomes more precise, allowing other visions to be realized as well.

## 3- FROM THE FAIRWAY

In golf the fairway is a good place to be. The grass is smooth and the golf ball sits up high, as you have a clear presentation hitting toward the hole.

Players can become over-confident in the fairway and sometimes get distracted and try to do too much with the next shot, hitting a less than satisfactory one. In the fairway it is important to retain your vision and focus.

In relationships, the fairway represents the good times.

Everything seems like it is perfect and will last forever. There doesn't seem to be a problem in the world as you and your partner enjoy the wonderful times.

But it is in the fairway that men can lose the focus of their visions and begin taking the relationship for granted, rather than keeping a deep sense of gratitude and appreciation.

This is an important time of empowering the visions you both share and honoring the process of the development and support of the relationship.

In relationships, feelings of gratitude need to be consistently renewed, and the fairway is the perfect place to accomplish this.

## Gratitude from the Fairway in Relationships

1- Promotion at work.
2- New baby.
3- New date.
4- Financial break through.
5- Goals being obtained.
6- Appreciating the partner you are with.
7- Proposal for marriage, getting married.
8- Being healthy.
9- Waking up and feeling alive and the abundance of life.
10- All the simple pleasures of life that can be taken for granted.
11- Being in love, and someone loving you.

Continue with this list with your partner:

12-
13-
14-
15-
16-
17-

18-
19-
20-
21-
22-

## Reflection:

Remember times in your life when you felt you were on the fairway and began to take your relationship for granted.

When on the fairway of life thank God for all your blessings each morning and evening and meditate on your vision.

## 4- IN THE ROUGH

In golf, the ball can land in thicker grass where it is more difficult to hit.

In the rough a player may not have as clear a shot to the green because of the position of the ball or perhaps trees blocking the way.

The rough in golf is not the best place to be, but it is a place on a golf course that may be encountered many times during a tournament. When in the rough, a player must retain his vision and concentration and bring his skills to a mastery level to win matches.

In golf, it is anticipated that all shots will not be perfect, but it is what a golfer accomplishes during difficult moments throughout the game that make the difference.

In relationships the rough represents difficult times and frustrating times. During difficult times in relationships you may think that you are with the wrong person; and you may become judgmental and critical.

As a golfer anticipates that the rough is part of the game of golf, partners in relationships ideally should have that same understanding.

**Being in the rough is part of the game.**

Then the rough in the relationship can be observed as a natural process of learning and growing and discovering new skills.

In the rough, partners will either see new opportunities where there are obstacles, or they will feel overburdened and not supported in the relationship.

If there is no open, compassionate communication during these times while discovering what the true frustrations are, the relationship will sink further into the rough, where both partners begin to distrust each other.

Many times in relationships, the symptoms of the problems are focused on rather than the real cause of the difficulty. If both partners lack the faith and love and strength to look deeply at the core level of the problem, then nothing truly changes and the rough continues to get more frustrating as time goes by.

If this occurs, it is an important time for both partners to receive assistance in order to regain their visions, and see what skills need to be developed to improve their game.

The rough cannot be avoided; it is part of the game of life and the nature of relationships. When partners learn to play in the rough, they can discover new levels of intimacy, and it usually will allow them to trust and appreciate the time in the fairway that much more.

## From the rough in relationships

1- Frustrations at work, at home.
2- Loss of job.
3- Not getting promotion.
4- Not feeling supported or loved.
5- Feeling disconnected sexually from your partner.
6- Not feeling turned on to your partner.
7- Sickness.
8- Desiring to be with someone else.
9- Feeling like your partner is not listening to what you are sharing.
10- Feeling like you are trying for things to improve, but things seem stuck.
11- Feeling betrayed or lied to.
12- Feeling like you're losing a sense of yourself expression.
13- Feeling judged or judging.

### Questions

1- In past relationships how have you responded to problems when in the rough?
2- How did you react to your partner?
3- What lessons have you learned when facing the challenge of being in the rough?
4- How do you and your partner communicate with each other when having to hit out from the rough?

Have you and your partner add to the list and share about these areas with each other.

1-
2-
3-
4-
5-

True spiritual growth and strength and trust develop when two people learn how to shoot out from the rough and feel like they do not want to hide anything from each other.

When you feel genuinely loved in the rough and feel absolute trust in your partner, your relationship can grow into the magnificent relationship you always desired.


## 5- In the Woods

The woods is definitely not a place a golfer wants to be, particularly if the golf ball is surrounded by trees with no clear shot to the green.

It can be one moment in a tournament where a player can lose everything. Just being in the woods can represent a lost stroke, though, if the golfer does not regain his vision quickly it can be a lost match.

The mental challenge in golf is enormous and the woods are definitely a most difficult place to be. If the golfer is masterful, he can reassess the situation quickly and focus on the next wise shot, getting out of the woods and back on the fairway. Sometimes players will attempt to hit through the trees toward the green, but remember if you miss this shot, the possibility of winning the tournament may seem hopeless.

The woods in the relationship represent very difficult times. The couple may feel hopeless. The vision they had for the relationship and trust in each other is gone and love has lost its light. The woods are dark and it seems that both partners have lost their way back to the fairway.


**If relationships never clearly get out of the rough, it becomes inevitable that the woods will be waiting.**

This is a time in a relationship where one person finally communicates the words:

"I believe we should end our relationship."

"I am in love with someone else."

"I think it is best that we separate, or divorce."

You may think the game is still going strong with more holes to play, but this is truly the time to wake up, for the game has been over for awhile.

In the woods, typically your partner feels like she has done everything she can to make the relationship work and feels now it is best to create a new vision with a new person.

If the power of the relationship has had a strong bond with deep love, it is possible to hit a hole in one. But remember holes in one do not happen very often, and if they do occur, the need of following through with consistent fairway shots would be absolutely necessary to bring an awakening to the relationship.

When insights occur in the woods, a possibility of opening a pathway back to the fairway is created. This can manifest into a deeper commitment and understanding of each other that can manifest into a hole in one.

### Insights from the woods in relationships

1- In the woods, you may discover aspects of yourself that were unrealized before. You may recognize how much you truly loved your partner, yet neglected to let her know or to support her requests and desires.

2- You may discover patterns about yourself that were manifested in other relationships and are still areas that you can improve.

3- You may discover, in the woods, where and how you lost your visions in the relationship and stopped expressing your powerful self.

4-    You may discover in the woods, that now you would be willing to do whatever it takes to improve the relationship. Yet it may be too late.

5-    You may discover in the woods, that in some mysterious way, even though you feel tremendous pain, loss, and sadness, that the relationship's end is for a higher purpose in the evolving of your life. And, that learning from the past and trusting God's ultimate plan is necessary.

6-    You may also discover that you may have done everything right and still the relationship ended in the woods, particularly if you were playing different games.

Insights you have discovered when in the woods in relationships.

Insights your partner has discovered. What did you learn about yourself?

1-

2-

3-

4-

5-

6-

7-

Questions:

1- What patterns about yourself have you seen in other relationships that did not empower the relationship?

2- When did you lose your vision, and how?

3- What would you be willing to do to rediscover and improve your relationship?

4- What have you discovered about yourself that

you weren't realizing before?

5- What is your vision for the future?

## 6- Sand Traps- Water Hazards

Sand Traps and water hazards on a golf course are all part of the game. Typically sand traps surround the green, and beautiful alluring ponds are positioned in front of greens.

Anyone who has played golf understands that part of the charm of the game is the unique course designs and the scenic beauty, that also often make the game more difficult. We all like challenges that test our skills, yet the object of the game is to avoid landing in the sand traps or water holes.

If a golf course were simply flat and boring, very few people would continue to play the game. Golfers want to be challenged in a way that brings out the best in them as they develop their mastery.

Sand traps and water hazards also test our focus and vision. They are temptations that can distract our eye off of the ball while being enticed by their very presence.

In relationships, sand traps and water hazards are distractions that can lure you away from your vision and commitments. These distractions test our strength and our faith and our commitment.

Couples often realize how strong their commitments to each other are when they are faced with distractions and temptations.

True committed relationships always remain clear in their integrity and love and respect that are shared with each other, regardless of the temptations.

How often has a golfer said,

*"I never would have hit the ball into the water if the water*

*wasn't there."*

*"As much as I tried to not hit the ball into the sand trap, I still hit it exactly where I didn't want it to go.*

When you are first mastering your game, it seems easy to believe that distractions caused you to miss your shot and lose your focus.

Though as you are improving you realize that distractions only occur when your vision is weakened by loss of concentration.

When relationships lose their powerful visions and dreams, it becomes easy for one or both of the partners to become susceptible to the attentions of someone outside the relationship.

When this occurs, it is important to regain your vision and discover what is important to you before you act out of impulse and land in a water hazard or sand trap. Traps are difficult to get out of and can hurt your score, as well as cause you to lose the game.

### Sand traps / Water hazards in relationships

    1-   In the business of life it is easy to forget simple promises you make to your partner

        a-   Pick up groceries
        b-   Call up the mechanic
        c-   Return items to store
        d-   Purchase tickets to the theater
        e-   Clean up the house
        f-   Be home at certain time
        g-   Remember specific events, or occasions
        h-   Remember your night out together

    2-  Temptations

        a-   Someone is attracted to you, and even though she knows you are in a monogamous relationship, she continues to express her desire to you.

b- Someone suggests you lie to your partner and keep something secret from her.

In relationships you should anticipate temptations as a normal process of life. Just like sand traps are part of a golf course, distractions are laid out in the course of your life.

### *Learn to keep your vision and your word:*

If you feel that the relationship has been in the rough too long, you may become susceptible to the charm of alluring distractions. Remember the rough is an important place for relationships to evolve into a deeper more meaningful experience. This is not the time to escape into someone else's arms, believing that the grass is greener and smoother on their golf course. Talk with your partner when you are feeling moments of temptation and discover the wonderful intimacy of working through thick grass together.

Distractions and temptations in your relationship- Write down which ones have occurred in your relationships. Have your partner share hers.

1-
2-
3-
4-
5-
6-
7-
8-
9-
10-

1-      What choices have you made in the past when

faced with distractions, or temptations?

2-      What are you committed to now in your life when distractions and temptations occur?

**When you are in a wonderful, evolving monogamous relationship, that has the potential to be the relationship of your dreams, and someone is admiring your golf clubs, golf balls, your driver, your putter's stance, or the hip rotation in your golfer's swing, learn to say, "No thank you, I'm in a great relationship." Anything less than that is an invitation to land in the sand trap. Once there, good luck with your pitching wedge!**

**" I had a chance with my putt at the last but I pulled it and gave him the match. It was a matter of picking the line and trusting it, but I pulled the putt."**

**Tiger Woods**

### 7- On the green- In the hole

The most difficult part of the game is played on the green. Where other shots on the fairway have room for error, the green is unforgiving. In golf the closer you get to the hole, the more mentally challenging the game becomes. A missed putt from a few feet away from the cup can leave a pro with a sinking feeling.

There isn't a moment to daydream on the green. Just a second of a lapse of concentration and a player can mis-hit a putt, and then still be faced with another putt, perhaps even more difficult.

The green is smooth, yet it can be allusive, with subtle curves and bumps. Learning to read the green is no different than learning to read the body language of your partner.

Beginning players tend to ignore practicing on the green, yet masterful players understand that every stroke has led to their finally seeing the ball land in that small hole.

In relationships, the green is represented by the consistent efforts that both partners have brought into creating a romantic and fulfilling relationship.

This is a time in relationships where serious questions regarding marriage or commitment or starting a family can be raised.

As wonderful as it is to be on the green, close to the hole, decisions may be manifested in various ways. In the relationship, the hole represents a completion or closure or decision that will effect the future of both partners.

On the green also requires patience. How often have you seen a golfer pace back and forth surveying the green before putting his shot? In relationships sincere, loving patience is necessary when you are faced with difficult decisions. This is a time of discussing with one another openly and honestly your feelings and thoughts that effect these decisions. When your partner feels your willingness to be patient, it will allow her to explore her concerns and fears, as well as her excitement, that may all be involved in her decisions.

If the vision of marriage has been a conversation for both partners since the initial tee shot, then the decision of that possibility is now staring at them three feet away.

The couple may decide they are still not ready for marriage, or one partner may decide that he or she has changed his/her mind, not about marriage in general, but marriage with you. Or, the sacrament of marriage may be the next shot, receiving it with joy and excitement and the feeling of a dream come true.

The green, like the fairway, should never be taken for

granted. Regardless of how many holes you have played together, if you have spent too much time in the rough, getting back into the fairway, and have even been in the woods without properly resolving issues; the green can be the place where both partners take one last look at each other, pick up their balls and clubs and walk separately to different golf courses.

In every relationship, big decisions always have us look deeply into ourselves, either welcoming the next shot going into the hole with blessed enthusiasm and committed love, or realizing something is missing, understanding that sometimes golf is a game you play alone!

### On the green decisions in relationships

1- Deciding to have a sexual relationship with each other
2- Deciding on a monogamous, exclusive relationship
3- Deciding on a committed relationship
4- Deciding to get married
5- Deciding on making the relationship work after being in the woods
6- Deciding on ending a relationship
7- Deciding on starting a family
8- Deciding on purchasing a new home
9- Deciding on moving to a different state
10- Deciding on a career change
11- Deciding on starting a new relationship

Make a list of decisions you are contemplating at the present time. How are you and your partner being patient with one another allowing thoughts and feelings to be explored and expressed?

1-
2-
3-

4-

5-

6-


When you are playing golf in your relationship, you want to be consistent. If you keep your initial vision your score will reflect a relationship that is growing and developing trust, respect, and love, and mutual support.

In the fairway remember to have gratitude and a perspective of all your blessings in life. When in the rough remind yourself to see the opportunities of learning when confronted by difficulties and frustrations. Couples can discover deeper intimacy at these times.

If that occurs when you are in the woods, a profound awakening can happen that can make a dramatic change in your lives.

## On the green fears and concerns

1- I am afraid sex won't be as great as I hoped.

2- I am afraid to be in a committed relationship. Maybe I will become more attracted to someone else.

3- I am afraid to get married- maybe it won't work.

4- I am afraid to give the relationship another chance, since I've been hurt too much already.

5- I am afraid to end the relationship. I don't want to hurt my partner and maybe I'm making the wrong decision.

6- I am afraid of starting a family. My whole life will change.

7- I am afraid to purchase a new home. I don't know if we can afford it.

8- I am afraid of starting a new relationship. I don't want to be hurt again.

## On the green excitement

1- I am looking forward to our sexual relationship feeling wonderful, and to our developing greater intimacy between us.

2- It is so exciting to be in a committed relationship. Being committed will open up pathways in my spirit I haven't known for awhile.

3- I am so excited to be getting married and being with the partner I am with. I am so blessed.

4- I am so excited that our commitment is deep enough to work through the woods and discover how much we love each other, and of our willingness to explore our thoughts and feelings.

5- I am excited about starting a family.

6- I am excited about purchasing a new home, especially with my partner, knowing that there is abundance in our life.

7- I am excited about starting a new relationship with new insights and understanding and passions for life.

If you come out of the woods with an opening in your spirit and heart, you may become clear of a divine plan beyond your own perception that is at work in your life.

**And remember when on the green, keep your faith. When the ball lands in the hole, regardless of what decisions you have made, it is time to begin creating visions for the next hole and the next fairway of your life.**

**"I think it could be a real advantage because I know the greens, they're tricky and hard to read sometimes."**

PGA Golfer Stewart Cink

### 8-Reading the Green

Since putting is so essential for the optimum score of a golfer, learning how to read the green is an artform all to itself. It can be both exciting and challenging, while you are discovering that any curve, bump, or deviation of any kind can affect the speed and direction of the ball heading toward the hole. Learning to read the green takes years of experience, and since each green is different, the challenge never ends. Your putt can even respond differently to the same green from day to day, depending upon how well the green has been cared for, and how it has been affected by the daily weather conditions, which also affect how the golf ball moves across its emerald grass.

Reading the green in relationships is reflected in observing your potential or present partner's body language. This also is an exciting and challenging expertise to develop. Body language may convey a silent self-portrait of stored experiences and memories, both wonderful and painful. This can be expressed through the tightness of one's muscles to the playfulness of one's smile. As well as how someone holds her posture, walks, and expresses herself when she communicates, which can reveal important information about her physical, emotional, mental, and spiritual attitude.

Anyone who has played golf knows that some greens are fast, while others are slow. Some are more flat, then bumpy. Some are unforgiving, while others more generous. Some greens are firm, others more soft, some bend to the right, others to the left, while some don't bend at all. Some greens sit on a lofty hill, some deep into a valley, while some are surrounded by water, and yet others maybe surrounded by trees.

Body language from one person to the next can be as different as the greens on a golf course. You may think that your putt is heading straight toward the center of the hole, yet at the last moment an unexpected dip curves your ball off to the right, missing the hole by two feet. You are standing there amazed and frustrated, feeling like you just read the green perfectly.

In relationships it isn't any different, as you are standing two feet away from your partner, feeling like you just missed a sweet putt, but not knowing how.

And then in an instant you see what you weren't aware of before. Your partner hasn't verbally communicated to you that she is troubled or upset, but subtle changes in her posture become evident that something is indeed wrong. Now in hindsight, you can observe the tension around her eyes and the tightness in her smile less receptive than usual. Her shoulders are turned inward, almost as if protecting her chest and heart. Maybe she was hurting. Her kisses are hard and fast, rather than soft and slow, and everything about her posture turns away from you, rather than toward you.

**Learning to read body language can help you improve the score of your relationship, particularly when you become aware of the subtle changes that occur day to day**.

When you are not reading your partner's body language effectively, it may seem that you and your partner are both playing golf but perhaps on different greens, and maybe even on different courses.

Observe your own body language and discover what information you are sending.

<u>Questions:</u>

1- When you are sharing about yourself, what does your body language convey?

2- When you are upset, how does your body language reflect that?

3- When you are attentively listening to someone, how does your body language communicate that to your partner?

Ask your partner what she observes at different times with your body language.

Share with your partner what her body language conveys at times.

# Relationship Athletics

## Golf Scoreboard

### Days

| | 1 | 2 |
|---|---|---|
| Hole in One | | |
| Lack of Vision | | |
| Clear Vision | | |
| Fairway | | |
| Rough | | |
| Definitely in Rough | | |
| Woods | | |
| Out of Woods | | |
| In Sand Trap / Water | | |
| On Green / In the Hole | | |
| Dunks | | |
| | | |
| | | |

| | | | | | |
|---|---|---|---|---|---|
| No Vision | 3 | Definitely in Rough | 3 | In Sand Trap or Water Hazard | 2 |
| Vision | 1 | Woods | 3 | On Green | 1 |
| Fairway | 1 | Out of Woods | 1 | In Hole | 1 |
| Rough | 1 | | | | |

In Golf, low score is optimum.

# Relationship Athletics

## Golf Scoreboard

## Days

| 3 | 4 | 5 | 6 | 7 |
|---|---|---|---|---|
|   |   |   |   |   |
|   |   |   |   |   |
|   |   |   |   |   |
|   |   |   |   |   |
|   |   |   |   |   |
|   |   |   |   |   |
|   |   |   |   |   |
|   |   |   |   |   |
|   |   |   |   |   |
|   |   |   |   |   |
|   |   |   |   |   |
|   |   |   |   |   |
|   |   |   |   |   |

| No Vision | 3 | Definitely in Rough | 3 | In Sand Trap or Water Hazard | 2 |
|---|---|---|---|---|---|
| Vision | 1 | Woods | 3 | On Green | 1 |
| Fairway | 1 | Out of Woods | 1 | In Hole | 1 |
| Rough | 1 | | | | |

In Golf, low score is optimum.

# Relationship Athletics

## Golf Scoreboard

## Days

| | 1 | 2 |
|---|---|---|
| Hole in One | | |
| Lack of Vision | | |
| Clear Vision | | |
| Fairway | | |
| Rough | | |
| Definitely in Rough | | |
| Woods | | |
| Out of Woods | | |
| In Sand Trap / Water | | |
| On Green / In the Hole | | |
| Dunks | | |
| | | |
| | | |

No Vision 3   Definitely in Rough 3   In Sand Trap or Water Hazard 2

Vision 1   Woods 3   On Green 1

Fairway 1   Out of Woods 1   In Hole 1

Rough 1

In Golf, low score is optimum.

# Relationship Athletics

## Golf Scoreboard

### Days

| 3 | 4 | 5 | 6 | 7 |
|---|---|---|---|---|
|   |   |   |   |   |
|   |   |   |   |   |
|   |   |   |   |   |
|   |   |   |   |   |
|   |   |   |   |   |
|   |   |   |   |   |
|   |   |   |   |   |
|   |   |   |   |   |
|   |   |   |   |   |
|   |   |   |   |   |
|   |   |   |   |   |
|   |   |   |   |   |
|   |   |   |   |   |

| | | | | | |
|---|---|---|---|---|---|
| No Vision | 3 | Definitely in Rough | 3 | In Sand Trap or Water Hazard | 2 |
| Vision | 1 | Woods | 3 | On Green | 1 |
| Fairway | 1 | Out of Woods | 1 | In Hole | 1 |
| Rough | 1 | | | | |

In Golf, low score is optimum.

"It is like a hungry man who never eats. Then he has a piece of bread. Then he has a sandwich. Then a steak, then he wants to go to the palace."

Guillermo Villas

On effects of winning

# Tennis

Tennis

Tennis- Two out of three sets

|  | 1 | 2 | 3 |
|---|---|---|---|
|  |  |  |  |
|  |  |  |  |

**"Winning never consumed Evonne Goolagong. She played tennis as though simply being on the court was the greatest joy in the world."**

**Billie Jean King**

1- Aces/ Winners
2- Double Faults
3- Lobs
4- Drop Shots
5- Baseline Hitting
6- Over Heads at Net
7- Singles/ Doubles

" I have an unbelievable fear of losing. That's what gets me going."
Pete Sampras

## 1- Aces/ Winners

Aces in tennis are powerful skillful serves that win points. And in tennis having a great effective serve is definitely an advantage in the game. The number one player in the world at the present time is Pete Sampras who is certainly known for his powerful serve, yet it is important to understand that aces alone cannot win matches. Like every sport many other skills are required to be playing your best.

Interestingly, one of the best players ever has been Jimmy Conners, and he has never developed an overpowering serve. Yet, he made up for it in every other way.

In woman's tennis, seldom is there an overpowering serve, which ultimately will win the match. And because women's serves are not as dominant, there are longer rally's that are more entertaining, and interesting to watch.

In relationships, men who hit aces are attractive, and seen as strong and charismatic. Aces are dominant characteristics that can manifest in positive successful behaviors that serve the relationship. But men who hit aces in relationships have to be careful not to overpower their partner, and not embarrass or intimidate their partner.

When aces are hit with understanding and compassion and the desire to improve and bring out the best in your partner, that can lead to couples discovering more passion and joy and connectedness in their relationship. There is sometimes a thin line between hitting an ace that serves your partner enhancing her skill and talents, verses attempting to hit an ace that does not serve your partner.

If your partner feels that the aces you are serving are always trying to improve her because she is not good enough, she may begin to look for another man to play with who may hit fewer aces, but enjoys all the strokes she already has.

When your partner feels her strokes are not good enough for you, nor will they ever be, regardless of how many lessons she takes, she begins to feel hopeless and resentful in the relationship.

### *ACES SHOULD ALWAYS SERVE YOUR PARTNER !!!*

**"Everything is flowing, and the ball is coming off my racket cleanly. If I've ever been in a zone, this is it."**
**Lindsay Davenport**

**Top tennis player**

## Possible Aces that Serve Relationships

1- Enrolling you and your partner in workshops or classes that create opportunities for you to enjoy learning and having fun together.

    a-  Dance classes
    b-  Relationship workshops
    c-  Personal growth workshops
    d-  Art classes
    e-  Meditation and yoga classes
    f-  Exercise classes
    g-  Spiritual retreats
    h-  Scuba diving classes

Add to the list, and have your partner add to the list also.

    i-
    j-
    k-
    l-
    m-
    n-
    o-

Enrolling your partner in creating healthy lifestyle habits that serve the relationship.

    a-  Exercising on a daily basis.
    b-  Going for walks together.
    c-  Reading and sharing thoughts with each other.
    d-  Brainstorming and masterminding with each other about goals and visions.
    e-  Healthy eating habits.
    f-  Meditating together.

Write other healthy lifestyle habits you would like to share with your partner. Have your partner write down habits she would like to share with you.

1-

2-

3-

4-

5-

6-

## 2- Double Faults

In tennis double faults occur also during serving. A player has two opportunities to serve a tennis ball to the other player. If both serves fail to be played properly, that is equal to a lost point, with a high percentage of double faults also leading to a lost match. In a relationship a double fault is equivalent to messing up, failing to learn from a mistake, being unwilling to change certain attitudes or behaviors, or lacking a desire to improve. This certainly can lead to your partner feeling hopeless in the relationship.

In tennis, if you can't get the ball into the other player's service box, then there isn't even an opportunity of engaging in the game and participating with each other.

Double faults can keep relationships from ever developing into intimate meaningful relationships.

In the beginning process of initial dating, double faults can end an evening with

"Thank you very much and good-night."

Obviously if you are learning to play tennis, learning to serve is extremely important.

In relationships, learning how to communicate with the

person you are with is the beginning of getting your serve across the net. If your partner, or date, feels you cannot do that efficiently and believes you don't want to, you may think you are playing the game, but the game has been over and the match ended before it began.

### *YOU MUST BE ABLE TO SERVE TO PLAY THE GAME !*

Double faults occur when you or your partner feels like something is not working well in the relationship and nothing is being done for the relationship to improve.

Relationships can be ignited to a new level of excellence if two people recognize certain patterns that are interfering with the development and depth of their intimacy. Sometimes seeing a counselor and taking a workshop together or even having a mutually respected friend listen to the problems you and your partner are having can help you gain an objective perspective and hit an ace. Sometimes this can initiate a deeper understanding of yourself, which may have you understand your partner more effectively.

Stubbornness or unwillingness to change can be the greatest double fault that keep a person from discovering the ultimate possibilities for an extraordinary, romantic, and exciting relationship.

If you're hitting double faults often, you simply need a few lessons to improve your game.

### **Possible Double Faults on Initial Dating**

1- Looking unshowered, unkept, unclean.
2- Being cheap.
3- Not being attentive in the conversation.
4- Talking too much- Talking too little.
5- Criticizing.

6- Being rude.
7- Flirting with other woman.
8- Forgetting her name.
9- Being too aggressive.
10- Being wimpy.

## Possible Double Faults in the Relationship

1- Unwillingness to change.
2- Resistance to new ideas.
3- Always wanting to be right.
4- Boredom.
5- Laziness.
6- Same routines.
7- Complaining and whining.
8- Criticism.
9- Always trying to fix your partner.
10- Lack of sexual interest.

Write out your double faults and have your partner write down what she believes would be a double fault.

1-
2-
3-
4-
5-
6-
7-

## Questions

1- How have double faults hurt your relationship in the past?

2- What are you doing to improve your serving game

and hit fewer double faults?


## 3- LOBS

Lobs in tennis are typically strategic shots that are hit during the course of the game. Lobs can be very effective when hit well, though in themselves do not always win points. Lobs can create situations on the court that can lead to winning a point. When lobs are hit too often, the game begins to move very slowly, and can become boring.

In relationships, lobs are represented as the downtime that all relationships require. This is a time when nothing spectacular is happening but the shared moments are being enjoyed with each other. This is a place where relationships rest and relationships nest. It is a time when the relationship can be recharging its energies, understanding that in a match, endurance and stamina are very important.

Yet if resting and nesting continues, where lobs are the only source of entertainment in the relationship, then the relationship can become fatigued and boring.

In tennis, lobs are effective, though too often and it can lose its uniqueness and the same can occur in the relationship.


*Too much down time can become a down relationship.*

### Possible lobs in relationships

1- Watching television- A little is relaxing, too much becomes boring.

2- Always eating in the house- It's nice to have cooked meals, but mix it up with fun.

3- Going to the movies- Very relaxing and fun entertainment, but be certain to be somewhere after and communicate and share your thoughts and feelings with each other.

4- Individual reading- This is important for each person to enhance his/her knowledge, simply remember to share thoughts and feelings with each other about what you're reading.

5- All routines in relationships can become lobs. Even sex can become routine and boring if there is not an intimate connection that empowers the relationship.

### *LOBS ARE GOOD, JUST MIX UP THE SHOTS !*

Write down possible lobs and have your partner add to the list also.

1-
2-
3-
4-
5-
6-
7-

**Questions**

1- What lobs would you like to do less?
2- How can you create the lobs in your relationship becoming more exciting?

### 4- DROP SHOTS

Drop shots are strategic shots in tennis. Sometimes, they are very effective and receive welcomed applause from the fans and other times they backfire miserably. They are amusing shots, not attempted too often, for it is the element of surprise that makes them effective. If someone knows you're going to hit a drop shot, the shot no longer serves its purpose.

In relationships drop shots are the cute surprises you spring on your partner. Sometimes they take the form of humorous jokes or gags or even the notorious surprise party.

Drop shots in relationships bring an element of fun and entertainment that can enhance the intimacy of the relationship. Yet when the surprise or joke backfires, it will not be appreciated as much as you hoped or anticipated.

A missed drop shot, or ineffective drop shot, at times can be costly to a relationship if your sense of humor and the element of surprise are not welcomed by your partner.

### Drop Shots in Relationships that Sometimes Work and Sometimes Don't

1- A surprise party-  You may have the best of intentions, yet if your partner is not in the mood for a lot of people, and entertaining at the moment, then it's a missed shot.

2- Bringing friends to the house unexpectedly.

3- Bringing a pet home unexpectedly.

4- Any gag or joke can be appreciated, yet if it embarrasses your partner, it can be a missed shot.

5- Sharing intimate details about your relationship with mutual friends that you thought may be cute, but your partner felt disrespected and embarrassed.

At a party, you are being very funny and entertaining. It's great if your partner enjoys your sense of humor and spontaneity, but if your partner feels embarrassed it can be a missed shot.

Drop shots can be effective and entertaining and enjoyed in relationships, particularly when you understand your partner's sense of humor and her probable responses to surprise. The goal of drop shots in relationships is to uplift the relationship, not to have your partner feel like you don't respect her feelings. If your partner has shared with you, how she dislikes surprise parties and you continually have them for her, your drop shots are missing the point, and heading toward a lost match.

Write down possible drop shots and have your partner write what she considers drop shots.

1-
2-
3-
4-
5-
6-
7-
8-
9-
10-

What drop shots have you attempted in the past that didn't work?

1-
2-
3-
4-
5-

**"It's harder to play Ivan Lendl than Boris because Ivan's more consistent, but if Becker's playing great, sorry, you have no chance."**
**Andre Agassi**

## 5- Baseline Hitting

In tennis the steadiness and consistency of baseline hitting is an intricate part of winning matches. It is the ability to be steady and chase down balls from backcourt and maintain a high percentage of skilled shots that keep the ball in play.

Two of the best players, Bigorn Borg and Chris Everett, were known for their baseline game and concentrated style. Both of these players hardly ever came to the net to volley a shot. Everything was hit from backcourt, hardly ever missing a shot, and firing winners when their opponents came to the net.

In relationships, baseline playing is the consistent, constant, and steady way you are that helps your partner feel secure, safe, respected and loved in the relationship. Good baseline playing scores many points and reassures your partner that she is not going to be loved today only to be criticized tomorrow.

When your partner feels that your affections are consistent, even when she is not perfect and messes up, her trust and openness in the relationship blossoms.

When your partner is feeling this supported by you, it allows her to be herself, sharing her deepest feelings with you, her hurts, her joys, her passions, and her dreams. As she is feeling this steadiness of your love, it is only natural for her to want to give you everything, possibly in a way that she has never been able to do before. Intimate conversations, sharing, and lovemaking all improve and open to deeper levels of commitment between both people. Couples who share this consistent bond trust in the longevity of their relationship and never see problems as something that can harm the relationship.

Baseline playing takes great patience and patience is necessary for relationships to develop into the romantic, passionate and long lasting experience partners are seeking.


## Possible Baseline Hitting

1- Being dependable
2- Keeping your word
3- Honoring and respecting your partner

4-   Being financially stable
5-   Thinking of your partners concerns and needs
6-   Being spiritually evolved and supportive
7-   If a parent- enjoying being a parent, dependable and consistent
8-   Being intellectually inspiring and creative
9-   A good sense of humor
10-  Feeling blessed about life
11-  Being attentive and understanding

Write down possible baseline hitting in your relationship and have your partner write down hers.

1-

2-

3-

4-

5-

## Questions

1. Where can you improve your baseline playing?

2- How have you seen your baseline playing improving over the last five years?

### 6- Overheads at Net

These strokes in tennis are the shots you patiently wait to receive, anticipating hitting an easy winner. Though on many occasions, instead of smashing the ball for a point, the shot is mishit and it becomes a lost point.

Since tennis is so often a game of quick reflexes, when the easy shot comes and the player has time to determine where he wants to hit the ball, a mishit can occur from having too much time to think.

In relationships, overheads at the net are represented by the wonderful gifts you receive from your partner, though at times you may fail to acknowledge and express gratitude for.

When your partner presents you with such a gift, you want to be consistent with your overhead shot and simply hit an easy winner.

Sometimes a simple thank-you is all that is necessary in relationships when you receive these gifts.

## *MISHITS AT THE NET ARE MISSED OPPORTUNITIES !*

### Overheads at Net in Relationships

1-    *Your partner buys you a gift.*
Express your sincere gratitude and appreciation of her love. Even if what she buys is not something you initially like, let her know how much you love her for thinking of you. You may decide that you like what she purchased later, which can often occur.

2-    *Your partner prepares a wonderful meal for you.*
Express your gratitude and be certain that you are not receiving her gifts as an expectation. Your partner may have labored with love to cook you a wonderful meal. Don't miss the opportunity to thank her.

3-    *Your partner puts on a sexy outfit.*
Be certain that you take notice and let her know how sexy and beautiful she is, and how she ignites the passions in you.

4-    *She has just had her hair done, or nails, or a*

*facial, etc.*

Be certain to notice and compliment her and let her know how beautiful she is and how much you love being with her.

5-    *She's dressing up for a formal party.*

Be certain you let her know how gorgeous she is and how she is your princess and how blessed you are to be with her.

6-    *She has created a romantic evening.*

Be certain to let her know how you appreciate the love and affection that she generously gives to the relationship.

7-    *She has created an afternoon picnic in the park on a beautiful day.*

Be certain to let her know how much you enjoy her uniqueness and how lucky you feel to be in her life.

8-    *She has plane tickets to go away for four days and desires to take you.*

See this as a wonderful opportunity for a romantic intimate time together. Let her know how much you love her.


So often men mishit these overheads at the net. Men need to learn how to compliment women sincerely. If it does not come naturally, then take lessons learning to hit overheads. Sometimes men can get distracted and mishit an overhead simply by not paying attention. Either saying the wrong thing, or saying nothing can be a mishit and a missed opportunity.

## Mishits at the Net

1- If your partner is wearing a new dress, a man may say, "Where did you get that, and how much did it cost?"

MISHIT

2- If a woman is wearing something sexy before going to bed. A man may say, " Were you planning something this evening?"

MISHIT

3- If your partner just had her hair done. A man may say, "Why did you cut your hair, or change the color?"

MISHIT

4- If your partner cooked a wonderful meal, and a man says, " Is there anything else for dinner?"

MISHIT

5- If your partner purchased a new sofa, or chair, and a man says, " Why did you buy that?"

MISHIT

6- If your partner begins being affectionate with you, and a man says, " Why are you doing that now?"

MISHIT

7- If your partner wants to plan a romantic getaway with you and you say, " I don't see why we have to go away"

MISHIT

8- If your partner just joined a spa to exercise and lose weight and you say, " I don't think it's going to work"

MISHIT

9- If your partner lights candles in the bedroom and wants to massage your body. And you say,"Can't we just have sex?"

MISHIT

10- If your partner wants to talk about marriage. And you say, " What's wrong with our relationship the way it is?"

MISHIT

11- If your partner wants to share something with you. And you say, " I don't have time."

MISHIT

**Mishits, or missed opportunities in a relationship are important for men to reflect upon, hopefully while still engaged in the relationship. Many times the reflections come after the game is over.**

How often have you heard someone say,
*" I can't believe I missed that shot. It was so simple. All I had to do was stick my racket out."*

How many missed opportunities have occurred in your past relationships and are still manifesting in your present relationship?

## Possible Missed Opportunities in Relationships

1- I can't believe I never told her how much I loved her.
2- I can't believe I never let her know how much she means to me.
3- I can't believe I didn't appreciate her every day.
4- I can't believe I didn't ask her to marry me.
5- I can't believe I didn't take her away on more vacations.
6- I can't believe I didn't listen to her more and find out what she was thinking.
7- I can't believe I didn't respond to her requests and desires.

Missed opportunities are excellent times for us to learn and evolve with a deeper understanding and insight so that in the future missed opportunities occur less as our score improves.

Write down mishits in relationships and share them with your partner and discuss how these shots can improve.

1-
2-
3-
4-
5-

**Mishits manifested by saying the wrong thing or not being observant about something can cause relationships to deteriorate quickly, yet hitting overheads is one of the easiest ways to score points and have successful matches and relationships.**

## 7- Singles / Doubles

In tennis, the game can be played in either singles matches or doubles matches. The strategies and personalities and skills of the games are entirely different.

In a singles match, the one player is responsible for everything on his side of the court. Every shot, every return, all serves will be performed by that one player. Your endurance, skill, focus, stamina, strength, and agility all have to be functioning at peak condition, for there is no one else to depend on. Whether the player wins or loses, there is no one else to give credit to and no one else to blame.

In doubles matches, you are sharing the court with another player. You both have to determine your strengths and weaknesses, evaluating the best strategy. You have to learn to depend upon your partner, as well as bring out the best in your partner. You also have to trust your partner and be certain you don't intimidate your partner when a mishit occurs.

In relationships playing singles is like being single and playing doubles is like being in a relationship.

When you are single, you can choose to do what you want when you want. You are not responsible for anyone else. When you are single, all your decisions only need to be addressed to one person; yourself. You understand if something needs to be done that you have to do it and if it is not done, then you are responsible. When single, you only need to take care of one person, yourself. When you are single, you can move freely all over the court, practicing many types of shots and serves and developing your own strategy for your life.

When you begin playing doubles, a relationship occurs, and now there are new rules. In relationships mutual boundaries are respected and assistance is expected, where now there is sharing of responsibility and sharing in decision making. The doubles players in relationships have to determine who is in charge of various areas and when to switch positions if necessary.

*In doubles, communication is crucial, and effective support and assistance when mishits occur is imperative.*

The last thing you want to do is isolate or overshadow your partner.

In doubles, as in the relationship, it is important not to blame your partner for mishits or lost points. Blame creates resentment and resentment leads to a doubles team becoming less effective.

On the court your goal is to bring out the best in your partner, so that she enjoys playing with you, and desires to play with you again, and finally forever.

Learning how to play doubles in order to win games takes time and practice and the same is true in relationships. We sometimes assume that we can get on the court and simply figure it out then, without any coaching or assistance or effort.

Watching the best doubles teams is like watching a work of art in motion.

*A problem occurs if you are playing like you're single when you're in a doubles relationship.*

1- Even though you have a wonderful partner to play with, you are always seeking out other doubles partners.

2- Telling your partner where to stay while you cover the rest of the court.

3- Getting angry when your partner misses a shot and somehow manages to get in your way on the court.

4- Constantly telling her how to hit the ball and where to serve.

5- Not introducing your partner to the other team.

6- Blaming your partner if your team loses and embarrassing her in front of everyone else.

7- If your team wins, even if you acknowledge your partner, she will be seeking a partner she can enjoy playing with. A partner who will truly appreciate her as a team mate.

## Playing Doubles in Relationships

1- Have a strategy.
2- Know each other's skills and talents.
3- Focus and concentrate, keeping your mind on the game.
4- Work together on the court, talking to each other.
5- Always appreciate and acknowledge good strokes and serves and insights.
6- Acknowledge mishits by reminding each other of the present point at that moment, understanding that each of you will occasionally have a mishit.

### *NEVER BLAME AND NEVER SHAME !*

7- Communicate when necessary in a positive way.
8- Be flexible with each other when it is necessary to change strategies.
9- Enjoy playing with one another and reminding yourselves how good it feels to be alive and playing this wonderful game.
10- Whether you win or lose, feel like you have played your best and have learned lessons that could only improve your game with each other.

## Questions:

1. Have you played singles in a doubles relationship before?
2. How did that affect the relationship?
3. Are you presently playing doubles more effectively with a present partner?
4. Do you feel like your partner enjoys playing doubles with you?

Ask your partner how your doubles game can improve creating more fun and shared experiences.

# Relationship Athletics

## Tennis Scoreboard

### Days

| | 1 | 2 |
|---|---|---|
| Aces that Serve | | |
| Aces that do not Serve | | |
| Baseline Hitting | | |
| Lobs | | |
| Overheads Missed | | |
| Overheads Made | | |
| Double Faults | | |
| Drop Shots Made | | |
| Doubles Good | | |
| Doubles Like Singles | | |
| | | |

| | | | | | |
|---|---|---|---|---|---|
| Aces that Serve | 3 | Overheads Made | 3 | Doubles like Singles | -3 |
| Aces that do not Serve | -3 | Double Faults | -3 | | |
| Baseline Hittings | 3 | Drop Shots Made | 2 | | |
| Lobs | 1 | Drop Shots Missed | -2 | | |
| Overheads Missed | -3 | Doubles Well | 3 | | |

# Relationship Athletics

## Tennis Scoreboard

### Days

| 3 | 4 | 5 | 6 | 7 |
|---|---|---|---|---|
|   |   |   |   |   |
|   |   |   |   |   |
|   |   |   |   |   |
|   |   |   |   |   |
|   |   |   |   |   |
|   |   |   |   |   |
|   |   |   |   |   |
|   |   |   |   |   |
|   |   |   |   |   |
|   |   |   |   |   |
|   |   |   |   |   |

| | | | | | |
|---|---|---|---|---|---|
| Aces that Serve | 3 | Overheads Made | 3 | Doubles like Singles | -3 |
| Aces that do not Serve | -3 | Double Faults | -3 | | |
| Baseline Hittings | 3 | Drop Shots Made | 2 | | |
| Lobs | 1 | Drop Shots Missed | -2 | | |
| Overheads Missed | -3 | Doubles Well | 3 | | |

# Relationship Athletics

## Tennis Scoreboard

### Days

| | 1 | 2 |
|---|---|---|
| Aces that Serve | | |
| Aces that do not Serve | | |
| Baseline Hitting | | |
| Lobs | | |
| Overheads Missed | | |
| Overheads Made | | |
| Double Faults | | |
| Drop Shots Made | | |
| Doubles Good | | |
| Doubles Like Singles | | |
| | | |

| | | | | | |
|---|---|---|---|---|---|
| Aces that Serve | 3 | Overheads Made | 3 | Doubles like Singles | -3 |
| Aces that do not Serve | -3 | Double Faults | -3 | | |
| Baseline Hittings | 3 | Drop Shots Made | 2 | | |
| Lobs | 1 | Drop Shots Missed | -2 | | |
| Overheads Missed | -3 | Doubles Well | 3 | | |

# Relationship Athletics

## Tennis Scoreboard

### Days

| 3 | 4 | 5 | 6 | 7 |
|---|---|---|---|---|
|   |   |   |   |   |
|   |   |   |   |   |
|   |   |   |   |   |
|   |   |   |   |   |
|   |   |   |   |   |
|   |   |   |   |   |
|   |   |   |   |   |
|   |   |   |   |   |
|   |   |   |   |   |
|   |   |   |   |   |
|   |   |   |   |   |

| | | | | | |
|---|---|---|---|---|---|
| Aces that Serve | 3 | Overheads Made | 3 | Doubles like Singles | -3 |
| Aces that do not Serve | -3 | Double Faults | -3 | | |
| Baseline Hittings | 3 | Drop Shots Made | 2 | | |
| Lobs | 1 | Drop Shots Missed | -2 | | |
| Overheads Missed | -3 | Doubles Well | 3 | | |

"We have to play hurt and cannot make mistakes in the field. We have to stay focused, stay fit, and stay hungry."

Irving Fryer

# FOOTBALL

| 1 | 2 | 3 | 4 |
|---|---|---|---|
|   |   |   |   |
|   |   |   |   |

**Football**

Four Quarters

1- Kick offs- kick off return
2- Complete Passes-Incomplete Passes
3- Touchdowns
4- First in ten
5- Fumbles
6- Quarterbacks
7- Tackling
8- Penalties
9- Out of Bounds

**"The greatest thing about sports is that it taught me that losing is not a terminal disease. Losing is nothing more than a life experience that should make you stronger, brighter, and better, to move further down the road."**

**Fran Tarkenton**

**" You learn from your adversity,**
**You learn from your mistakes,**
**You learn from your losses probably**
**More than you do from the**
**Winning and successes."**

**Fran Tarkenton**

## 1-Kick off/kick off returns

In football kick offs and kick off returns begin the game, occur after scores, and begin each quarter. This sets the tone for the game and determines where the first play will begin on the football field.

Good kick offs are necessary, as are good kick off returns. They typically do not win games but without them no game would get started.

In relationships kickoffs and kick off returns can be related to your first dates or first day on a vacation or other initial events with each other.

If you do not have an impressive kick off on your first date, then there probably will not be a responsive kick off return manifesting into a second date.

On a first date if you are communicative, friendly, respectful, polite, and interested in the other person's thoughts and opinions, then the likelihood of that person being receptive to you is enhanced greatly.

If you do not execute a good kickoff on a first date, you may want to get some coaching in this area, since it will be difficult to gain yardage in the game if you can't get the ball moving.

You may be a great quarterback once you get into the game but the initial kick off is essential for the other person to desire to play with you.

### Kickoffs in relationships on first date

1- Meeting at an accepted comfortable place.
2- Open friendly communication.
3- Eye to eye contact.
4- Expressing yourself authentically and just being yourself.
5- Sharing about aspects of your life, relating about

the past as well as the future.

6- Listening attentively to the other person.

7- Light-hearted stories.

8- Appreciating what she shares with you and enjoying the differences and similarities between you.

9- Being polite and generous.

10- Being genuinely interested in who she is so that she feels open and safe in your presence.

11- Having fun.

## Positive kick off returns

1- The time tends to go quickly as one conversation naturally leads to another

2- Her body language becomes more open and relaxed as the time goes by.

3- You don't feel rushed on your first date; instead you sense a feeling of spontaneity as you are sharing with each other.

4- Her communication becomes more expressive, particularly as she shares about herself.

5- You sense she is interested in you by the questions she asks you.

6- You sense that she does not want the date to end, that she is enjoying your company

7- There is shared laughter.

8- By the end of the date, a follow-up date seems only natural.

9- If you hug her or hold her hand, you can feel her receptiveness to your touch.

10- After a short time you discover you share some common interests and common goals.

11- You are looking forward to seeing her again and she has shared a similar feeling with you.

## 2-Completed passes-Incomplete passes

In football, one of the most beautiful plays in all sports takes place. It is the completed pass. As the quarterback and wide receiver align their signals, it takes the form of a choreographed ballet.   The communication between the players seems telepathic. Of course some passes are missed, either from poor execution or confusion in the communication, but when it manifests, it is poetry in motion.

When completed passes occur, it can be for a touch down or to bring a team closer to scoring. When the pass is incomplete, no yardage is gained and no yardage is lost, though it can cause frustration, making it more difficult for a team to win.

In relationships, completed passes empower the partnership between each other. Both of you are communicating the same play and having the same desire to complete it. When the pass is caught, not only does it gain yardage for the relationship but it also creates momentum and excitement heightening the chances for more yardage to be gained and touchdowns scored.

When there is an incompleted pass in the relationship, one or both partners can be left with a feeling of frustration.

Notice that when several attempted passes or several attempts at communication fail, both partners may choose to call more running plays, avoiding conversations that seem difficult. This would be like running away from important unresolved issues.

Avoiding throwing certain passes in relationships may occur when you do not want to confront uncomfortable conversations which in turn can cause you to lose the game.

At the same time, if the conversations open up the possibility for a completed pass, the couple may discover a deeper commitment and have more fun, while learning to use the whole field, understanding that passing and running in the right direction are necessary to win the game.

When completed passes occur, an acknowledgement is

acceptable and appreciated.

" Thank you for catching my pass."
"Thank you for throwing your pass."

**Completed passes strengthen relationships when requests are honored by each other.**

## Completed Passes in Relationships

**1st Partner:** "I threw the ball right to you, just like we agreed. Why didn't you catch it?"

**2nd Partner:** "I told you before, I don't like to catch footballs, and you're still throwing too hard."

**1st Partner:** "I'm sorry I'm still throwing hard. I want to learn to throw easier, though I thought we agreed it's important for our relationship to score points and win the game, as we learn to pass and receive."

**2nd Partner:** "Well, there are other ways to score points and win the game. I've just never liked catching the passes. They're just too confrontational."

**1st Partner:** "Well, I definitely want us to win the game and passing is an essential part of it. I promise I will throw easier. Can you promise you'll attempt to catch my pass?"

**2nd Partner**: "Well, I love you, and I want us to win the game, too, and I know how I avoided catching passes in my past relationships; and that never worked for scoring touchdowns. I promise I'll give my best, if you try to be more compassionate and understanding."

**1st Partner:** "Thank you for just now catching my pass. I appreciate when you are willing to change to help us score and I promise I will improve."

**2nd Partner:** "Thank you for throwing a beautiful pass and not letting me run away or choosing to run away yourself. I appreciate when I feel your commitment for us to win."

**1st Partner**: " I love you."

**2nd Partner**: " I love you."

**"The encouraging thing is we didn't play as well as we can and we won. But we've got to get better at some things."**

**Dan Reeves, Falcons Head Coach**

What are some complete passes in your relationship?

1-
2-
3-
4-

What have been some incompleted passes in the relationship?

1-
2-
3-
4-

Create a dialogue with your partner that allows an incompleted pass to become a completed pass.

### 3- Touchdowns

In football, touchdowns score points and win games. Typically it takes many plays to score touchdowns, and throughout an entire football game not that many touchdowns are made.

Touchdowns are the result of perseverance, consistency, mental and physical toughness and the ability to push forward even when you are hurting.

Football is a game played without excuses. It is played in the cold harsh winters, when it is raining, and even when it's snowing. It is a game where the players understand the price that has to be paid in terms of pain and fatigue in their commitment to scoring and winning.

Touchdowns in relationships assist in developing strong deep committed partnerships. Couples, in scoring touchdowns, learn that not everything is going to be easy, and at times life can be difficult. These are relationships committed to winning the game regardless of the pain and hurt. Men who are willing to run for touchdowns also know that the joyous celebration of commitment is always possible.

Men who score touchdowns are strong in their character and persistent in their love and devotion.

Men who are willing to score touchdowns are self-sacrificing, even when their partner manifests weakness. Men who score touchdowns will also be forgiving, expressing the depth of their commitment to such a degree that their partner will be awakened to her own personal emotional and spiritual growth.

When scoring touchdowns, men are not afraid to dig deep within themselves, knowing that they will find a way to succeed regardless of what is occurring at the moment.

**Women appreciate a man who is willing to stand by her,**

**not only in the good times but also through all the storms on the playing field.**

### Possible Touchdowns in Relationships

1- Weathering illness
2- Weathering loss of investment
3- Weathering loss of jobs
4- Weathering a miscarriage
5- Weathering loss of child through illness or accident
6- Weathering partner's possible addiction problem
    a- alcohol
    b- drugs
    c- anorexia
    d- bulimia

7- Weathering partner having an affair
8- Weathering partner lying or deceiving
9- Weathering partner's various moods

In our relationships it is important to understand that each one of us is developing and evolving in our own spiritual growth. In the process of this manifestation we are all going to fumble at times. When we are able to weather these storms, we often experience a depth of love that was previously unknown to us.

Write down touchdowns you have scored in the past.

Have your partner share her touchdowns. Share touchdowns others have scored for you.

1-
2-
3-
4-
5-
6-
7-

Share with each other the feeling you would have knowing your partner was willing to weather any storm for you because of her devotion and love.

## 4-First and Ten

As teams advance down the field to the goal trying to score touchdowns, they have an opportunity of making first and tens. This allows a new set of plays each time the team advances ten yards. First and tens are absolutely necessary to win games.

In relationships, first and tens create new opportunities to change and evolve.

As long as a relationship has first and tens, the relationship is moving forward in the right direction toward the goal that the couple is envisioning.

With every first and ten comes new enthusiasm, renewed passion, restored faith and the reassurance of playing with each other.

Couples who create consistent first and tens seldom become bored with each other. They are focused on their relationship and the goals they share all the while enjoying passing the ball back and forth to each other to obtain those goals.

## Possible First and Tens in Relationships

1- Going on vacations, or short weekend outings with each other.

2- Taking workshops or seminars together or separately and sharing the information with each other.

3- Taking educational classes and being willing to continue learning.

4- Taking classes or lessons together that bring excitement, fun, and intimacy into the relationship.

A- Dance classes   (All kinds of dancing)
B- Art classes
C- Golf lessons
D- White water rafting or kayak lessons
E- Gardening classes
F- Fishing lessons
G- Singing or music lessons
H- Add your own, everything and anything that is fun

5- First dates leading to second dates, and eventually conceiving a possible future with each other.

6- Meeting friends and family members of your partner and creating new friendships.

7- Playing games together and sports together.

## Questions:

What first and tens are manifesting in your relationship?

What first and tens would you like to create?

1-
2-
3-
4-
5-
6-
7-


## 5-Fumbles

Fumbles in football are costly, for if you lose possession of the ball, you lose the opportunity to score points and win games. Fumbles are like errors. They can change the momentum of the game, and sometimes are difficult to recover from. Fumbles in football can occur anytime, anywhere, any moment, even when things are going great, and you're only five yards from the goal line.

Of course some fumbles are worse than others, depending upon the score of the game and how much time remains.

Fumbles in relationships also can occur any moment. If a fumble is bad enough, getting back possession of the ball can be hard and the relationship can suffer the consequences.

The more fumbles that do occur the more the relationship will be weakened, until it is almost impossible to score touchdowns and win.

Fumbles can happen on first dates or in marriages that have been developed for years. If a few fumbles occur on a first date, there probably will not be another first and ten and the game will be over.

If you can recover your own fumble immediately and take responsibility for dropping the ball, that can certainty cause less of a problem in the relationship than if you lose possession of the ball.

Men need to learn to apologize when they have fumbled so

that their partner feels not only understood but also respected. Recovering your own fumble can create thoughtful, responsible, intimate conversations that deepen the bond between both partners.

If a man seldom or never recovers his own fumble, nor accepts responsibility for dropping the ball, his partner may begin to feel hopeless in the relationship, determining that he either doesn't care or he is insensitive to her feelings and desires.

### Possible Fumbles in Relationships

1- Being insensitive to your partner.
2- Flirting with other woman.
3- Embarrassing your partner.
4- Not listening to her when she is sharing something with you.
5- Not honoring her requests.
6- Not assisting her with house responsibilities and children responsibilities.
7- Being sloppy.
8- Being rude.
9- Making decisions that effect the both of you without asking her thoughts.
10- Making other people and circumstances more important than your partner.

When you recover your own fumble, acknowledge how your action hurt your partner and apologize authentically.

"I am sorry I embarrassed you the other night. I'm sorry that I hurt you. I do not want to hurt you. I am committed to our relationship becoming stronger, and it is my desire not to hurt you."

"I am sorry I did not help you with the chores yesterday. I know that does not empower our relationship when I do not keep my word with you."

## Serious Fumbles in Relationships

1- Lying
2- Cheating
3- Resisting  changing destructive behaviors
4- Unforgiving
5- Dominating
6- Controlling
7- Judging

## Recovering from a Serious Fumble

I am sorry I lied to you.

I know how that damages our relationship.

I promise that I will not lie to you again.

I know that right now you may not believe me, since I have lied to you in the past.

I understand that, and I know it may take time for you to regain your trust in me.

I am committed to this relationship, and I am committed to improving and doing anything you desire to have our relationship become stronger.

I am sorry I hurt you.

It hurts me, knowing how I hurt you.

I do not want to lie to you ever again.

I love you.

When you recover your own fumbles, then touchdowns, and winning the game are still possible goals to achieve. Games are lost when men do not recover their own fumbles.

**Have you and your partner write a recovering letter, if necessary**.

I am sorry that _____.

I know how that affected our relationship

_____  _____.

I know right now, you are still hurting

_____  _____.

I know it may take time

_____  _____.

I am committed to our relationship

_____  _____-.

I  am willing to do these specific actions to regain your trust

and strengthen our relationship

_____  _____.

I am sorry I hurt you

_____  _____.

I promise that  _____  _____.

I love you.

**"What makes him comfortable is his home, and his kids and every day life, not being put on a pedestal, not being called a hero every five minutes."**

**Jennifer Montana**

**Referring to her husband star
Quarterback Joe Montana**

## 6-Quarterbacking

In football everything is centered around the quarterback. Quarterbacks in football are in charge and lead their team either to victory or defeat. Quarterbacks have to be focused, agile, spontaneous, and in command at all times.

Great quarterbacks know how to empower the rest of the team so that the whole team is functioning as one.

Great quarterbacks make quick decisions based on what is occurring at the moment, even when there is a specific play in motion.

Women are drawn to quarterbacks because of their versatility and leadership.

Football teams can win football games only if they have a good quarterback who can throw a touchdown pass, or choose to run, or hand off to someone else to gain yardage.

## Quarterbacks in Relationships

Quarterbacks like to be in charge and run the plays and create strategies in the relationship. This can be a wonderful trait as long as the quarterback remembers the most important aspect of the game is to empower and share with his partner.

While quarterbacks will get most of the attention on the playing field and in the relationship, it is essential that they recognize the importance of the other players and their partners in the relationship. If there is not that admiration, the team will lose, and the relationship will fail.

Since quarterbacks have so many talents and skills, they have to remember not to overshadow their partners or boast about their triumphs. Successful quarterbacking only occurs when your partner feels like she is part of the team and that her love empowers you to be even a greater quarterback.

### Successful quarterbacking in relationships

1- Sharing responsibilities in the relationship and always being ready to take care of whatever is necessary. Quarterbacks never procrastinate; putting things off for another day. Quarterbacks are involved in every play.

2- Always willing to see his partner's point of view, and always willing to bring out the best in his partner.

3- Spontaneous, and willing to change plays. The willingness to do what makes the team move forward and score touchdowns.

4- Having specific goals and visions for the development of the relationship.

5- Positive, energetic, healthy, and abundant attitude. An attitude that is focused and compassionate, and loving in the relationship.

### Not successful quarterbacking

1- Dominating
2- Stubborn

3- Controlling
4- Selfish
5- Demanding
6- Egocentric
7- Judging
8- Overbearing

## Questions:

What are some positive quarterbacking skills you are manifesting in your relationship?

1-
2-
3-
4-
5-

What has been negative quarterbacking in your relationships?
1-
2-
3-
4-
5-

Share with your partner how these qualities affect the relationship and how more successful quarterbacking can occur.

**Ask your partner if she will assist you in becoming a greater quarterback.**

## 7-Tackling

In football it is necessary, when playing defense, to tackle the player who is attempting to gain yardage. Literally, defense means stopping the offense from moving forward. The defense's job is to keep the other team from scoring.

In relationships, tackling can be manifested as being overly possessive and protective and attempting to control and stop your partner from moving forward.

Relationships develop specific patterns after awhile and sometimes both partners are running the same play again and again. When your partner wishes to change and explore a new strategy or possibility, you may feel like you want to tackle her at the line of scrimmage feeling threatened by her desire to discover something new while changing from the consistent routine.

Tackling can interfere with the natural evolving and development of a relationship. It is important that each person in the relationship feel the freedom to improve in all aspects of their life. When a woman is with a man who is possessive, it is very difficult for her to become fully expressed and feel truly loved for who she is.

Men who are tacklers may need assistance exploring their own insecurities, for this manifestation does not allow your partner to be the best player she can be.

### <u>You know you are a tackler if:</u>

1- You are overly possessive.
2- You are overly controlling.
3- You want to make all decisions.
4- You don't feel your partner's needs or desires are important.

5- You feel like you have to be the better player on the team.
6- You feel like your partner should think just like you.
7- You don't think your partner should want to change or learn new things.
8- You have to be right.
9- You are resistant to change.
10- You're overly jealous.

Write down tackling that has occurred in your relationships.

1-
2-
3-
4-
5-
6-
7-
8-
9-
10-

How has tackling interfered with developing deeper joy and intimacy with your partners?

Have your partner share with you where she believes tackling exists in your present relationship.

## 8-Penalties

Penalties in football cause teams to lose yardage. Like fumbles they can also cause a team to inevitably lose a game.

Whereas in fumbles you may lose possession of the ball, penalties typically have you retain the ball but make it more difficult to score.

In relationships men have to become acutely sensitive to hear when a whistle has blown and there has been a penalty.

Sometimes the penalty whistle will be quiet and subtle, yet other times it can be loud and clear. Sometimes men do not know what they have been penalized for or do not even know that there has been a penalty. This will make it extremely difficult to score points. Particularly as each penalty is pushing them further backfield, causing them to lose valuable yardage, actually moving away from the goal.

Penalties will be different in different relationships. In one relationship your action or behavior may be a first and ten, yet the same actions in another relationship may be a penalty.

Also penalties change within the same relationship. What may have scored points initially, can become a penalty later in the relationship. Unless men learn to listen to whistles being blown and know when a penalty is occurring, it's impossible to score touchdowns.

Men understand when they fumble a ball and lose possession or recover their fumble but penalties can be very frustrating and confusing, particularly when they don't understand the penalty.

Men may think that a certain play should have received a first down, rather than a penalty. Men can become very uncertain of themselves at this time in the relationship, specifically when they have no idea that a penalty has happened.

Some penalties are more obvious than others, such as speaking disrespectfully to your partner or forgetting an important date causing a penalty to be called.

Often you will know you have committed the offense and your best comment would be:

*"OK, I know I did it, how much yardage am I losing, and what can I do to make up for it?"*

Penalties, like fumbles can happen at any moment, even when things appear wonderful. Because women sometimes call

167

penalties silently, it is extremely important for a man to know how his partner communicates penalties and scores points. It would be a good idea at this time to review your initial scouting report to determine your partner's past communication style.

Relationships that end with a man believing that the relationship was improving, and he was scoring points, and throwing touchdowns, and was on track to win the Super Bowl, was a relationship where a man was penalized more than he can imagine. Maybe some penalties he was aware of, though there were probably many plays where the whistle was blowing for a loss of yardage while he thought he was catching touchdown passes.

**Possible penalties that may not be verbally communicated often come under the heading of:**

### THE NOT ENOUGH SYNDROME

1.    Not outgoing enough

2.    Not handsome enough

3.    Not wealthy enough

4.    Not spontaneous enough

5.    Not well mannered enough

6.    Not energetic enough

7.    Not healthy enough.

8.    Not successful enough.

9.    Not spiritual enough.

10.    Not generous enough.

11.    Not romantic enough.

12.    Not casual enoughNot formal enough.

13.    Not good enough lover.

14.    Not good enough father.

15.    Not smart enough.

16.    Not strong enough.

17.    Not creative enough.

18.    Not loving enough.

19.    Not friendly enough.

20.    Not old enough.

21.    Not young enough.

22.    Not thin enough.

23.    Not athletic enough.

24.    Not sexy enough.

When the final whistle blew and the game was over, he realized he had not advanced pass the fifty yard line, even though he thought he was holding the Super Bowl ring in his hands ready to share it with his partner. He had actually lost the game due to penalties that fall into the not enough category. If couples do not communicate and work through these "not enough" feelings, their relationship will eventually lose so much ground that it is difficult to get back in the game much less score touchdowns and win.

## Penalties in Relationships

1- Anything that annoys, irritates, or angers your partner.

2- Penalties change with time and change in different

relationships.

3- Penalties may be expressed or suppressed.
   **Penalties are costly in relationships**.


Make a list of penalties that you have been charged for in past relationships, in your current relationship. Include those that fit into the "not enough" category.


1-

2-

3-

4-

5-

6-

7-


**Ask your partner each day if there have been any penalties. Be willing to listen without making any defensive moves.**


## Questions:


1- Which ones were you aware of and which ones were you not?

2- Discuss with your partner the style you both have used in determining and communicating penalties.


### 9-Out of Bounds

In football running out of bounds is a strategic maneuver to stop the clock. Of all the plays discussed in this book, attempting to get out of bounds and buy some time occurs only in football. When the clock stops, that, too, gives the team time to regroup and set up a new play with the hopes of gaining yards and possibly scoring a touchdown.

In relationships stepping out of bounds is like setting up specific boundaries. When your partner communicates that she feels like her boundaries are being disrespected, she will step out of bounds to stop the clock and stop the motion of the relationship.

At this point, when your partner is sharing her boundaries with you, she is attempting to set up a new play that could result in a touchdown. She may be willing to discuss alternative plays with you. However, the game cannot continue until you mutually agree on the next play and ultimately the direction of the game.

When you neglect to understand the communication of your partner's boundaries, you are setting yourself up for fumbles and penalties.

Your partner or potential partner may begin to feel that you simply don't care about her boundaries, particularly, after you both have set up a new strategy in the huddle.

Boundaries are different for different people, and also change in the relationship. On a first date if you try to gain yardage quicker then your partner wishes, she will immediately step out of bounds, stopping the clock. At that moment you have time to create a new play and move downfield a little slower or the game may end rather abruptly.

It is important for us to have boundaries, and important to respect and honor them. As a relationship develops trust and intimacy boundaries naturally begin to change.

## Possible out of bounds in relationships

1- Too aggressive on first dates
2- Expecting to know about someone's private life before you have gotten to know them
3- Not putting things away like your partner requests

4- Opening up your partners mail
5- Overly jealous, wanting to know everything the other person does
6- Possessiveness
7- Dominating and controlling behavior

## Questions:

1- How have you responded when your partner has stepped out of bounds and stopped the play?

2- Do you feel like your partner feels supported in the relationship enough to share what her boundaries are?

**Have your partner share with you where she has felt her boundaries were ignored or disrespected.**

1. Anything that your partner or potential partner feels that disconnects her from the relationship is an out of bound.

2. When your partner steps out of bounds and sincerely communicates to you, LISTEN!

## Possible Out of Bounds Communications

1- "I like you, but I feel you are wanting to score too quickly."

"Thank you for sharing that with me, I'll move one yard at a time, if you wish."

2- "I feel like you don't respect me at times, and honor my requests."

"Thank you for sharing that with me for I do want to be the best quarterback for you."

3- "I'd rather not have sex tonight. Can you just hold me?"

" I would love to hold you. Simply feeling you in my arms is so wonderful to me."

4- "I felt judged by you the other day and I've been angry."

" Thank you for sharing that with me. I'm sorry I _____.
I love you. You are the light of my day. I want to score touchdowns with you."

5- "I'm sad. I feel like our relationship is stuck at the fifty yard line and not moving forward."

"Thank you for sharing that, I believe we have both been so busy, we've stopped completing passes and getting first and tens. Lets go away and have a romantic, intimate weekend and renew our visions with each other. I love you."

**Stopping the clock and communicating out of bounds is essential for relationships  to score TOUCHDOWNS and WIN THE GAME.**

# Relationship Athletics

## Football Scoreboard

### Days

| | 1 | 2 |
|---|---|---|
| Touchdowns | | |
| Fumbles Recovered | | |
| Fumbles Not Recovered | | |
| Penalties | | |
| First and Downs | | |
| Kick Off Good | | |
| Kick Off Bad | | |
| Tackling | | |
| Complete Passes | | |
| Incomplete Passes | | |
| Out of Bounds | | |
| Quarterback Good | | |
| Quarterback Not Good | | |

| | | | | | |
|---|---|---|---|---|---|
| Touchdowns | 4 | Kick Off Good | 2 | Out of Bounds | 0 |
| Fumbles Recovered | -1 | Kick Off Not Good | -2 | Quarterback Good | 4 |
| Fumbles Not Recovered | -4 | Tackling | -2 | Quarterback Not Good | -4 |
| Penalties | -3 | Complete Passes | 2 | | |
| First and Ten | 3 | Incomplete Passes | -2 | | |

# Relationship Athletics

## Football Scoreboard

### Days

| 3 | 4 | 5 | 6 | 7 |
|---|---|---|---|---|
|   |   |   |   |   |
|   |   |   |   |   |
|   |   |   |   |   |
|   |   |   |   |   |
|   |   |   |   |   |
|   |   |   |   |   |
|   |   |   |   |   |
|   |   |   |   |   |
|   |   |   |   |   |
|   |   |   |   |   |
|   |   |   |   |   |
|   |   |   |   |   |
|   |   |   |   |   |

| | | | | | |
|---|---|---|---|---|---|
| Touchdowns | 4 | Kick Off Good | 2 | Out of Bounds | 0 |
| Fumbles Recovered | -1 | Kick Off Not Good | -2 | Quarterback Good | 4 |
| Fumbles Not Recovered | -4 | Tackling | -2 | Quarterback Not Good | -4 |
| Penalties | -3 | Complete Passes | 2 | | |
| First and Ten | 3 | Incomplete Passes | -2 | | |

# Relationship Athletics

## Football Scoreboard

## Days

| | 1 | 2 |
|---|---|---|
| Touchdowns | | |
| Fumbles Recovered | | |
| Fumbles Not Recovered | | |
| Penalties | | |
| First and Downs | | |
| Kick Off Good | | |
| Kick Off Bad | | |
| Tackling | | |
| Complete Passes | | |
| Incomplete Passes | | |
| Out of Bounds | | |
| Quarterback Good | | |
| Quarterback Not Good | | |

| | | | | | |
|---|---|---|---|---|---|
| Touchdowns | 4 | Kick Off Good | 2 | Out of Bounds | 0 |
| Fumbles Recovered | -1 | Kick Off Not Good | -2 | Quarterback Good | 4 |
| Fumbles Not Recovered | -4 | Tackling | -2 | Quarterback Not Good | -4 |
| Penalties | -3 | Complete Passes | 2 | | |
| First and Ten | 3 | Incomplete Passes | -2 | | |

# Relationship Athletics

## Football Scoreboard

## Days

| 3 | 4 | 5 | 6 | 7 |
|---|---|---|---|---|
|   |   |   |   |   |
|   |   |   |   |   |
|   |   |   |   |   |
|   |   |   |   |   |
|   |   |   |   |   |
|   |   |   |   |   |
|   |   |   |   |   |
|   |   |   |   |   |
|   |   |   |   |   |
|   |   |   |   |   |
|   |   |   |   |   |
|   |   |   |   |   |
|   |   |   |   |   |

| | | | | | |
|---|---|---|---|---|---|
| Touchdowns | 4 | Kick Off Good | 2 | Out of Bounds | 0 |
| Fumbles Recovered | -1 | Kick Off Not Good | -2 | Quarterback Good | 4 |
| Fumbles Not Recovered | -4 | Tackling | -2 | Quarterback Not Good | -4 |
| Penalties | -3 | Complete Passes | 2 | | |
| First and Ten | 3 | Incomplete Passes | -2 | | |

## *WHEN THE GAME IS OVER*

## *AND*

## *BEGINNING A NEW GAME*

"The game has emerged from the grave with thunder. You don't hear about the strike anymore. Sometimes something has to almost die, like baseball did for the miracle to take place."

> **Felipe Alou**
> **Manager**
> **Relating to the 1998 Baseball season**

" What Ali and I need to do is get together as soon as possible and kiss each other. We should embrace. We should talk, and we should laugh together. Then we both need to forget about all those things that happened in the past, its over."

Joe Frasier

Regarding Muhammed Ali

## WHEN THE GAME IS OVER

In baseball traditionally there are nine innings; though they may sometimes go into extra innings. Tennis is played in sets, and typically two out of three sets wins a match. Golf is played through eighteen holes, though there can be four rounds in a tournament. Basketball is played in four quarters, though sometimes it can go into overtime, and football is played in four quarters.

Regardless of the sport, when the game is over, it is over! As much as a player wants to, he can not replay a shot or a pitch or a putt or pass. If a fumble caused a game to be lost, or an error allowed two runs to score, the player ultimately was responsible for the outcome of the game.

Typically anyone who has ever played a sport and lost a game understands that how we lose and what we learn are the most crucial aspects of the sport. If we learn the wrong lessons, or learn nothing at all, we continue to repeat the same mistakes.

Initially when the game ends we may be in disbelief or denial. The look on Karl Malone's face when again Michael Jordon and the Bulls won the NBA championship expressed it all. It seemed a moment before, the game was Malone's to win, and then in a blink of an eye, Jordon's magic prevailed, leaving Malone with a look of confusion, shock, and horror. We can only imagine how many times Malone and his team, the Jazz, played those last thirty seconds in their minds, wondering how they let the victory slip away.

In relationships, how often have you said,   "I was just getting warmed up;  my slump is over; I have found my vision again;  just give me the ball one more time;" just to realize that not even a hole in one or grand slam could miraculously save your relationship.

If you had been in a relationship for awhile, you may have felt that you were still gaining yardage and getting first and tens. You may have been willing to play with the physical and emotional pain necessary to reach your goal, not realizing that she was playing golf and was not as willing to endure the pain as you, and not as committed to play in any weather conditions.

In your disbelief and denial that the game has truly ended, you will have the tendency to still behave as if there will be another opportunity to swing the racket or another chance to chip onto the green.

But once denial begins to fade; anger, sadness, and loss will all begin to manifest. And it is important for your spiritual growth that you evolve through these phases of pain.


**"Anytime you lose it's no fun. I made some mistakes. Hopefully I'll learn from them."**


**Peyton Manning**
**Rookie Quarterback**


No athlete plays a sport to lose, yet inevitably someone does lose, and feels the agony of defeat, particularly if that athlete has given his best, attempting to pitch his greatest game, desiring to play his heart out, running back and forth on the basketball court, or starring into the hot sun, after the last serve in tennis is called out by the lines people.

In a relationship you may feel impulsive urges to be combative and confrontational, yet when the game is over, no matter how you argue with the umpires, it will not get you back in the game or the relationship.

Regardless of how angry you feel, thinking certain penalties and fouls were unjust and unfair, acceptance of the loss is necessary for you to move forward and eventually prepare for the next tournament.

Typically in sports, it is easy to blame everything and anything when you lose. Bad calls, distractions, fatigue, sore muscles are just a few.

**"It's hard. It's not easy to accept. It's the same when we lost with the Cubs in 89. It's a terrible feeling."**

**Greg Maddux**
**After Losing in the 98 Playoffs**

Losing with honor is a valuable lesson in sports, discovering where your game needs to improve, while feeling you gave your best in this particular match. Blaming or looking for excuses will not help you improve your game. True champions always rise to the occasion and take responsibility for their performance, regardless of the outcome of the game. In relationships blame is a natural process to move through, as you are feeling your anger and loss. However, when you are feeling rejected from the game, blaming your partner seems natural.

### Question:

1- How have you blamed your partner for ending the game?

**After losing, even great athletes may feel so depressed that they just want to throw in the towel.**

**"I felt if I had to give my life to make the World Series I would do that but our destination was to make it to the playoffs and that was it."**

**Sammy Sosa**

Sometime after feeling your anger, you may want to escape and throw in the towel. This can be a difficult time and certainly a time of reflection. During my own separation and process of divorce, I came face to face with a desire to disappear from everything I knew. And so I share this with you at this time.

I felt I had to escape. My sense of purpose in life was gone. Everything that I had worked toward now seemed meaningless. I needed adventures that would have me forget everything. A friend who had traveled throughout the world shared with me his journeys and experiences. And the more he did, the more I realized there was nothing keeping me here. My marriage had failed and I had to get away. Even if it were just for three months, maybe that would be the escape I needed.

So I did it.

For a month I traveled thorough Africa. I had always dreamed of the adventures of a safari and now it was happening. I woke with the lions and grazed with gorillas and watched the elephants playfully bathe in muddied streams.

Another month I trekked through the mountains of India and shared meditations with other soul-seekers. Then I flew to Spain and hitchhiked along the countryside. Then scouted medieval castles in Portugal. Then eventually for weeks wrote poetry in Italy and France and shared stories with new faces and new friends.

Yes, I had escaped. Yes I had many adventures. Yes I almost learned to forget my pain and sadness. Yes it was a dream fulfilled. But there was one thing I could not forget at all. It stayed with me each day and night. It lived and hounded my dreams. It was reflected in the eyes of strangers and reflected in the spirit of animals. As I gazed into the nighttime stars and as I sensed the ethereal passing of clouds, I was constantly reminded of my children.

I wondered how they were doing; what they were thinking. I realized for me, these three months had been a time of discovering a new spark in my soul yet for them who were still so young, how each day was passing with experiences that held the possibilities of transformation and how ultimately these moments shaped their destiny.

And I realized that I was not there as a father to assist them in their decisions, and not there to share in their celebrations, and not there to love them through their difficulties. And I realized after these months of escaping from the world of pain that I missed being there with them, and being part of their lives each day that was evolving each moment.

And as I sat there deep in my meditative thoughts, I could see a light illuminating through the passageways of my mind, and I could feel a soulful smile resonating inside the abyss of my spirit. A deep breath lifted pass my tension as I could feel a new breath of life filling me with purpose and vision once again. And in that one moment of eternity, I was thankful that these months of travelling and escaping were only a few moments in the magic of my imagination. As real as it appeared, I thanked God that I had not missed the precious rhythms of time with my children.

Maybe travel and adventure will be part of my destiny but not as an escape from my family, or myself, but more from a place of healing, that never sacrifices my children.

So tonight I would be there to share in the stories and in the prayers, to listen to any of the complaints of the day, and I would feel the simple, wondrous blessing of being a Dad.

**"I was at my low. I was ready to quit. I never in my life thought about retiring until this year about when it was going to be."**

                                        **John Smoltz**
                                        **Atlanta Braves Pitcher**

## POSSIBLE EXPRESSIONS OF BLAME AND ANGER

1-    I am angry that she ended the relationship.
2-    I am angry that she did not communicate more to me and express her feelings.
3-    I am angry, how she has chosen to end the relationship.
4-    I am angry, since I felt our relationship was improving and I wanted to be with her forever.
5-    I am angry that she does not answer my phone calls or letters, and chooses not to talk with me.
6-    I am angry that she is already involved in another relationship.
7-    I am angry since I feel our relationship now was insignificant, and meaningless.

8-      I am angry that she has broken up our family.

9-      I am angry that I will not be able to be with my children every day.

10-     I am angry that she lost faith in our relationship.

Once you begin taking responsibility, you may discover that perhaps you didn't hit as many singles as you thought you did, and perhaps, you stopped throwing touchdown passes, and sinking foul shots, and perhaps you lost your own vision as the relationship fell into the rough, and never truly recovered.

Perhaps, as you walk off the field you begin to realize that you and your partner were playing different sports with different balls, and even if you would have pitched a perfect game, the relationship may have ended, particularly if she was playing tennis and you were playing football. When the game is truly over, it is imperative to regain your vision, enabling you to discover what spiritual lessons are available to you that will empower you to be a better player in relationships.

As you are reading this book and playing the games in it, observe how easy it can be to create an extraordinary romantic, fun, and long lasting relationship.


## <u>REGARDLESS OF HOW YOU FEEL</u>

1- Be kind to your partner, and be kind to yourself.

2- Learn from the game and discover what you would do differently in the next game, and what qualities you would want in your next partner.

Review the EVALUATING YOUR PARTNERsection in this book.

3- Understand the process of evolving, learning, and healing, and know that God's plan may be difficult for you to see at this moment. Just know and believe. It is a great plan filled with lessons of life.

4- Create a healing and forgiving heart and spirit. Forgiving yourself as well as forgiving your partner for any actions that damaged the relationship, and the on going friendship.

5- Forgive your partner for ending the relationship.

6- Respect your partner's requests.

7- Create your new vision. You may be pitching tomorrow.

Eventually you want to remember the game you played with your partner in a positive way. Regardless of how the game ended, whether if was by a strikeout, a foul, or a penalty, the relationship gave you many gifts that are to be part of your own spiritual journey that improve your game in the future.

## POSSIBLE GIFTS FROM YOUR PARTNER

1- She assisted me in my career.

2- Her expression of love allowed me to communicate more freely.

3- Her knowledge stimulated me intellectually.

4- Her creative spirit had me become more creative.

5- Her positive attitude had me see the beauty in life daily.

6- Her smile and laugh opened my heart.

7- Her intuitive wisdom stirred my spirit.

8- We brought children into the world and shared parenthood.

9- We fulfilled many goals together.
10- We traveled together and shared life's experiences.
11- She opened her heart to receive my love.

Write down your own gifts you have received from relationships that have ended.

1-
2-
3-
4-
5-
6-
7-

What gifts do you believe you gave your partners to take with them?

1-
2-
3-
4-

*We ultimately learn and evolve through our weaknesses.*

How did you contribute to the relationship not working? What errors, mishits, or fouls occurred?

1-
2-
3-
4-
5-
6-

Remember a time in your life that was difficult in which it seemed impossible for a comeback to occur, yet something wonderful and extraordinary did take place with time.

*Sometimes our sadness and loss can contribute to our greatest insights, triumphs, victories and spiritual healing, connecting us with God.*

In sports, players cannot improve unless they have someone to participate with. We learn, evolve, and improve while playing the game, discovering our strengths and weaknesses. Every athlete improves when his standard of excellence increases.

In relationships you also improve and discover what you truly desire and how you can make a difference in creating the most passionate romantic relationship. Be thankful for partners who have shared your life.

**Thank You Letter**

Dear_____,

Thank you for being in my life. Thank you for giving your love and tenderness to me and sharing with me the treasures of your soul, your past, your dreams, your pains, and your joys.

Thank you for participating in my life and contributing to

me in many wonderful ways that allowed me to express myself to learn and grow.

Thank you for being there at times when I needed you, and other times for just being present with me in laughter and love.

# Beginning a new game.


"When God makes someone, the most important part is the heart and soul.   What's on the outside is only decoration."


**Muhammed Ali**

"Give me golf clubs, fresh air, and a beautiful partner, and you can keep the golf clubs and the fresh air."

**Jack Benny**
**Comedian**

## Sexual Attraction in Sports and Relationships

There is definitely sexual attraction and charismatic presence that athletes manifest. As spectators we are drawn to their power, agility, the firmness of their bodies, their passion, and their commitment toward excellence.

In relationships there is also sexual attraction and charismatic presence that may entice you toward someone. The way someone looks, the scent of her skin, how she moves her arms, how she walks, the gestures of her face, and how she communicates, can all bombard your senses simultaneously.

Sometimes you can become so intoxicated with the lure of one's sexual attraction that you will forget to properly evaluate the person based on the qualities that may be more important for an intimate, romantic, trustworthy, and lasting relationship.

Once again you may find yourself enjoying the way someone easily glides across the tennis court, though they may be incapable of hitting out from the rough in golf. You may be attracted to how forcefully they can dunk a basketball, yet their percentage in foul shooting is very low. They might have a homerun swing of the bat, yet be unwilling to hit consistent singles.

Relationships just manifested on a sexual attraction will not be able to endure slumps and errors and fouls for too long and the relationship will suffer the consequences relatively quickly.

Too often other qualities about someone may be ignored, simply because

" Someone feels right"

How often have you heard someone say

" I don't know what we have in common, or what visions we share, but, I just know it feels good."

Sexual attraction typically occurs because of uniqueness about someone, or simply the newness of the relationship, or a certain charisma that person manifests that arouses you.

In sports, the feel of a racket or a golf club is essential for a player's performance. When you find the right golf clubs or bat or tennis racket, it feels like a relationship made in heaven. It feels like it was designed for your body, but if you did not know how to play golf, or tennis, the club or the racket would make little difference in your game. And so it is the same in relationships.

**Though feeling good is essential, in sports and in relationships, it is not enough.**

If you are sexually attracted to someone, *be able to know what feels good* to you about him or her.

1- The way she communicates to me feels good.

2- The way she treats me feels good.

3- The way she touches me feels good.

4- The way she listens to me feels good.

5- The way she is generous feels good.

6- The way she honors and respects me feels good.

7- The way I feel protected with her feels good.

8- The way she holds my hand feels good.

9- The way she says my name feels good.

10- The way she is patient feels good.
11- The way she is sincere and honest feels good.
12- The way she kisses me feels good.
13- The way she expresses her emotions and thoughts feels good.
14- The way she enjoys life feels good to me.

**Remember Broken Bats, Tennis Rackets, and Golf Clubs are easier to replace than relationships.**

### Questions:

1- In your past relationships did the initial sexual attraction interfere with the development of the other essential qualities that you desired?
2- What happened after some of the sexual magnetism wore off?
3- What insights do you now have about this?

Have an open conversation sharing this with your partner.

Review evaluating your potential partner or present partner on a regular basis.

Write ten things you are willing to change immediately to improve your mastery in relationships.

1-
2-
3-
4-
5-
6-

7-
8-
9-
10-

1- If you are going to hit more singles, be specific. How? When? Where?
2- How are you going to avoid fouls?
3- How are you going to know if a penalty has occurred?
4- How are you going to know if you hit a homerun, or had an assist, or ace?
5- How are you going to behave and communicate when in the rough?
6- How often are you going to play a sport in the relationship?

**Every great athlete after losing a game has to rediscover his zone and move forward regarding his vision and positive attitude.**

## Positive Affirmations

1- I am a great single hitter
2- I love to hit homeruns
3- I love scoring points
4- I am a consistent foul shooter
5- I am a great quarterback
6- I love to serve aces
7- I have a great baseline game
8- I love completing passes
9- I appreciate being in the fairway
10- I look for opportunities in the rough

| 11- | I love seeing my visions completed and fulfilled |
|---|---|
| 12- | I love to hit overheads |
| 13- | I enjoy creating triples |
| 14- | I am a team player |
| 15- | I am a great rebounder |
| 16- | I love to assist my partner |
| 17- | I like throwing touchdowns |
| 18- | I am willing to create a first and ten |
| 19- | I am responsible for my errors and strikeouts |
| 20- | I am a Sosa, McGuire homerun hitter |
| 21- | I love to play doubles |

## Switch Hitting in "Relationship Athletics"

Once you have played relationship athletics through all the sports, now have fun switch-hitting. Each day the woman will score her scorecard evaluating how she believes she has done. At the same time her partner will score his score card evaluating how he believes his partner has done. At the end of the day go over the score card with each other while having fun sharing with one another. At the end of one week discover even deeper intimate, wonderful changes in the relationship, and choose your next sport.

*Have fun playing the games, and have fun becoming the best player you can be!*

The most difficult part of writing this book has been sinking the last three-foot putt in the hole. As I mentioned in the introduction of this book, I have been a student of "Relationship Athletics", and I have enjoyed the process of learning and playing, as well. Hopefully as you participate in "Relationship Athletics" you will gain insights and fun while creating the relationship of your dreams.

Please feel free to share, your experiences, insights, holes in one, grandslams, renewed visions, touchdowns, completed passes, and rebounds that are assisting your relationships.


**"When you talk about 70 you're getting beyond the realm of reality and into the realm of SHOELESS JOE JACKSON coming out of the cornfield."**

**Bob Costas, announcer, referring to Mark McGuire's homerun record of 70 home runs**
**In reference to the movie, <u>Field of Dreams</u>.**


MY WISH TO ALL OF YOU IS FOR YOU TO EXPLORE AND TO DISCOVER YOUR **FIELD OF DREAMS...**

## "Terms for Relationship Athletics"

1- **Playing the field-** Still seeing what possibilities are existing while you are dating.

2- **Choking under pressure-** Stresses in life that have you lose your vision.

3- **Stealing-** Cheating on your partner.

4- **Walking-** Getting on base, but boring

5- **Coming to the net-** Being assertive.

6- **Double play-** Scoring two ways in one act or gesture.

7- **Coming from behind-** When you decide to change, the relationship can improve.

8- **Going to bat for me-** Protecting and defending the person you love.

9- **Touching base-** Communicating with your partner.

10- **In a Huddle-** Making a decision.

11- **Video Replay-** Discussing what really happened.

12- **Monday night quarterbacking-** Going over what you would do differently if you could do it over again.

13- **Coming through in the clutch-** Meeting all your expectations and more.

14- **Fast Break-** Ending a relationship quickly.

15- **In the zone-** Your passion is on fire.

16- **Half time/ Seventh Inning Stretch-** Evaluating the relationship and discovering where you want to go from here.

17- **Eye on the ball-** Keeping your vision and attraction toward your partner.

18- **Sandtraps/Water hazard-** Alluring Distractions.

19- **Swish-** Perfect

20- **Screen-** Honoring and Protecting.

21- **Three pointer-** Smart, sexy, successful

22- **In a Rundown-** Either way can be good or bad.

23- **Running out the clock-** Letting the relationship wind itself out.

24- **Covering all the bases-** Certainty of your information before communicating.

25- **Field of Dreams-** Perfect partner/soul- mate.Vision

26- **Scoring-** Winning points in the relationship.

27- **Crossing signals-** Confusion in conversation.

28- **Offsides-** Inappropriate behavior.

29- **Lay up-** Smooth and charming

30- **Foul Ball-** Another Chance.

31- **Slicing-** Lying.

32- **Reading the green-**Observing someone's body Language.

33- **Completed Pass-** Excellent Communication.

34- **Fumble, Error, Foul-** Messed up.

35- **Out of Bounds-** Stopping the play to talk.

36- **Tackling-** Interfering with your partner's desire to change and learn new things.

37- **Lobs-** Routine- laid back

38- **Drop shot-** Amusing, though could back fire.

39- **Rebound-** Another Chance.

40- **Dunk-** Aggressive.

41- **On the green-** Near completion.

42- **Fairway-** Gratitude.

43- **Blocked shots-** Fear, defensiveness

44- **Triple-** Willing to stretch deep to empower the relationship

45- **Jump ball-** Making Decisions

46- **Sosa, McGuire-** Major Grandslam.

47- **Slump-** Out of your zone.

48- **Hole in one-** Miracles, Blessing, Fantasies

49- **Out of the woods-** Awakening

50- **Quarterbacking-** Leading

51- **Strikeout-** Missed Opportunity

52- **Single, Points-** Consistent good action.

53- **Foul shots-** Expected wonderful qualities in  a committed relationship.

54- **Wild Pitch-** Dangerous behavior

55- **Ace-** Powerful behavior

56- **Double Fault-** Not learning from your mistake.

57- **The ball is in your court-** It's your decision.

58- **Overhead-** Gifts

59- **Touchdown-** Scoring Big

60- **Dunker-** Self Centered

61- **On the same field-** Playing the same sport where communication is understood.

## More " **If Relationships were like Sports**" to Come

I am in the process of writing other books that will allow us to discover new insightful ways to have fun using the dynamic of "Relationship Athletics".

If, after reading this book, and playing "Relationship Athletics", you are discovering your relationship improving to new wonderful levels of passion and intimacy, please let me know. With your permission your stories may be shared in future books.

What ongoing singles or points have you been scoring? What triples or grandslams have occurred? Have you had any holes in one or amusing drop shots? How has your quarterbacking improved, and what mishits, fouls, or errors have you been avoiding? And of course any other "Relationship Athletic" insights you have explored, please share those as well. I look forward to reading them.

Just send them to:

Dr. Marty Finkelstein
Sol-Rose
4292 D. Memorial Drive
Decatur, Ga. 30032

Or call
404-292-6786
FAX- 404-292-7384

I also can be contacted at this address for speaking engagements, information about future books, workshops, and audiotapes.

You can order additional books by contacting Dr. Marty Finkelstein.

## Dr. Marty Finkelstein

Dr. Marty Finkelstein has been a holistic chiropractor since 1980 specializing in physical, emotional, and spiritual wellness. He has hosted and produced "To Your Health", a cable TV show, and hosted "Wake Up To Your Health", an a.m. radio show. He is the author of several books, and articles and he continues to be a motivational educator who inspires others to seek optimum healing and wellness in their lives. He is the creator of several workshops including

*Healing Oneself Through Separation and Divorce*
*Healing Relationships*
*Relationship Athletics* based on this book
*Waking the Creative Spirit*

Dr. Marty has been the chiropractic representative for Flying Doctors of America travelling to other countries delivering chiropractic care and faciliting healthy communication and understanding between allopathic and holistic professionals.

Throughout Dr. Marty's life, three things have been consistent and are still present, **Relationships, Sports, and God.**

# About the Author

Dr. Marty Finkelstein has been a holistic chiropractor specializing in physical, emotional, and spiritual wellness. He has hosted and produced "To Your Health" a cable T.V. show, and hosted "Wake Up To Your Health", an A.M. radio show. He is the author of several books and articles, and continues to be a motivational educator who inspires others to seek optimum healing and wellness in their lives. He is the creator of several workshops including: "Healing One's Self Through Separation and Divorce"

"Healing Relationships"

"Relationship Athletics".

Dr. Finkelstein has been the chiropractic representative for Flying Doctors of America travelling to third world countries delivering chiropractic treatment.

CPSIA information can be obtained at www.ICGtesting.com
Printed in the USA
LVOW060217100212

267979LV00001B/40/A